Dedicated to my son

Michael Conor Neall

About the Author

Lucinda Neall has worked for many years training organisations in teambuilding, motivation and communication. When she became a parent she found the communication strategies at her disposal stood her in good stead with her teenage stepchildren but did not give her all the tools necessary to deal with her younger son. The missing ingredient was provided by Faber & Mazlish's 'How to Talk so Kids will Listen' which Lucinda and her husband used to set up a study group before going on to train other parents in these methods.

Having run courses for school managers on how to get the best out of their staff, Lucinda wondered to what extent the communication skills she taught would be useful in the classroom situation. She asked some of the headteachers she had worked with if she could spend time observing how teachers communicated with their pupils, then designed and ran courses on 'Classroom Communication' and 'Communication for Self-Esteem'. Whilst coaching teachers on how to use these skills Lucinda noticed that some had difficulty in engaging some of the livelier boys in their classrooms, and she decided to investigate what motivates boys and how teachers could communicate in a way that brings out boys' best qualities. From this research came 'Bringing the Best out in Boys'.

Lucinda enjoys working with young people and has founded the Leighton Buzzard Youth Arts Festival, set up the Leighton-Linslade Youth Forum and runs her local youth club.

BRINGING THE BEST OUT IN BOYS

Communication Strategies for Teachers

Lucinda Neall

Illustrated by Kate Sheppard

Hawthorn Press

Published by Hawthorn Press, Hawthorn House,
1 Lansdown Lane, Stroud, Gloucestershire, GL5 1BJ, UK
Tel: (01453) 757040 Fax: (01453) 751138
email: hawthornpress@hawthornpress.com
Website: **www.hawthornpress.com**

Cartoons and cover illustration by Kate Sheppard
Photographs by Lesley Fox
Cover design and typesetting by Hawthorn Press, Stroud, Glos.
Printed by The Cromwell Press, Trowbridge, Wilts.

British Library Cataloguing in Publication Data applied for

ISBN 1 903458 29 3

Contents

Acknowledgements

My thanks go to the teachers who let me observe them, who told me about their experiences with boys, and on whom I tried out these ideas; to the teachers I heard about but did not meet, whose winning ways were enthusiastically described by their pupils and colleagues; to all those who provided me with information and examples; and last but not least to the boys themselves who candidly told me how it is for them.

Thanks also to all those who encouraged me along the way, especially those who read and so helpfully commented on the draft manuscript at its many stages.

I would also like to acknowledge Adele Faber and Elaine Mazlish whose work on talking to children has inspired and guided me, and the people who provided me with the support I needed to get from first draft to publication: Lesley Fox, Deborah Hawkins, Jean Hitchen, Rachel Jenkins and my husband Peter Neall.

Foreword

Ted Wragg, Professor of Education at Exeter University

Girls have begun to outperform boys in virtually every subject. Back in the mid 1980s there was less than one percentage point difference between the numbers of boys and girls obtaining five high-grade GCSEs at the age of sixteen. By the beginning of the new millennium the gap had grown to ten per cent: 55% of girls secured this passport to jobs, and entry to higher levels of education, compared with 45% of boys.

This yawning gulf might matter less were it not for the rapidly changing world of employment. During the 1970s and 1980s millions of jobs disappeared from manufacturing industry, as car plants, steelworks and other giants that had recruited massive numbers of young male school leavers each year into traditional 'muscled' jobs reduced their workforce or closed down. Nor was there any sign of a reversal in this trend: who was going to get rid of two fork lift trucks and hire ten unqualified young men with big biceps instead?

As new jobs replaced old ones the future pattern of employment became more clear. Rapidly expanding fields involved working with people: hospitality (catering, hotels, restaurants, fast-food take-aways); care of the young, the sick and the increasing population of elderly citizens; communication with the public via newspapers, radio, television, interactive services, public relations.

In the early 19th century one third of the population worked on the land; today the figure is less than two per cent. We are witnessing a parallel to the industrial revolutions of the past, but instead of leaving the fields to enter factories, people leave factories to work with their fellows. Employers increasingly seek recruits who have good interpersonal skills and are clutching a decent GCSE in English. Over two thirds of girls obtain a grade of A* to C in English, but barely half of boys do so. The odds against boys getting a decent job are rising substantially.

As the 21st century dawned the alarming nature of the differences in outcome of boys' and girls' schooling became clear. Girls in pre-school groups talk to each other, so vital language skills are already being honed. Boys at this age are more likely to specialise in sound effects, roaring round the room in an imaginary Formula One racing car. In primary schools girls outperform boys in reading and writing, but that is not new. What is more novel is that boys as a group do not catch up later. In secondary schools they fall behind in virtually every GCSE subject, they do less well at A-level, are less likely to get into university and nowadays obtain fewer top class degree results.

The position is no better at the lower end of the achievement scale. The great majority of pupils leaving school at sixteen without a single graded GCSE are boys. Their behaviour in school is also worse. Fifteen times more boys than girls are excluded from primary schools for bad behaviour, while in secondary schools the figure is over four times higher. Whether one considers high or low attainers, classroom behaviour or academic achievement, boys as a group now come second.

Yet we still offer socially constructed stereotypes as reason and justification for these statistics, just as happened with girls in the

1970s. Two or three decades ago it was widely believed that girls were largely airheads who lost interest in education once they acquired a boyfriend, wanting to leave school at the earliest opportunity to become secretaries and hairdressers. Now the equally talented daughters of these apparent no-hopers are doing extremely well at school and university. Instead people stereotype boys as the feckless ones, interested only in playing football and going out with their mates. This current stereotype is as artificially constructed and negative in its impact as its predecessor.

The way ahead is not for society to wring its collective hands, lament the hopelessness of trying to interest young adult males in further study, or simply walk away from the problem as if there is nothing to be done. My own research projects have unearthed many examples of successful practice that can be generalised. We found that in the 5-7 age range three quarters of mothers, but only half of fathers, read with their children. During the 7-11 period it was half of mothers, but only a quarter of fathers. Many schools have tried to involve family males – fathers, brothers, uncles, granddads – in reading with children, signalling the clear message that reading is important for both males and females. One six-year-old boy we studied improved enormously when his granddad bought him comics and his father read books with him. Another 10-year-old boy changed from hating reading to loving it within one year, because his teacher gave him books on sport, adventure and humour which he enjoyed far more than the pale froth he had been offered previously.

Feminists used to say that girl-friendly schooling was also boy-friendly schooling. Exactly the same can be said in reverse. Nothing that any school does should take away from girls. They may have achieved spectacularly in the last twenty years, but there is still much to do. Four or five times more boys than girls study for A-level physics, so sex stereotyping has not gone away. By creating conditions that help boys' behaviour and motivation to improve, life in classrooms can be made pleasanter for girls too.

This book makes a notable contribution because it tries to tackle the issues in a positive way, without reducing opportunities for girls. Its emphasis is on positive steps that teachers can take. If we do not approach the education of boys in an optimistic and imaginative manner, we risk leaving whole sections of the community to emerge under-educated, having achieved less than their true potential. That would be a tragedy for the whole community, not just for those boys who miss out.

Ted Wragg

Introduction

Peter Downes, Homerton College, Cambridge

Scarcely a week goes by without a reference in the press to the under-achievement of boys in schools, or to their loutish behaviour, or to their rampant criminality. Many of society's current problems are laid at the door of the failure of schools to provide an adequate and successful education for a substantial proportion of its male population. The sense of alienation among many (but by no means all) young men represents a serious threat to our future social stability. That is why this book is important – it contributes significantly to the growing wealth of experience about how this problem may be tackled effectively.

Until a few years ago, many teachers pretended that the problem did not exist, or they were simply unaware of the growing gap between the performance of boys and girls throughout the educational process and particularly at 16. 'Boys mature late but they catch up by A Level', was the general platitude used to dismiss any concern expressed. More recently a number of factors have combined to sharpen the thinking: the publication of SATs results, examination league tables and the increased emphasis on academic performance in the assessment of individual teachers' performance and payment.

Awareness of the problem has become general and is now well documented in many publications, references to which can be found in the bibliography. Indeed, the very length of the bibliography bears witness to the determination of the teaching profession to find a solution. There is however no simple solution: a wide range of techniques is now being used and action research based in schools is developing our understanding of the key issues.

The generally accepted wisdom is that boys are getting an increasingly raw deal in the earliest years of their life, those crucial first five years when talking and reading are established, together with habits of concentration and patterns of play. Not that parents of male children are deliberately seeking to victimise them – far from it. What seems to be happening is that the general trends in society – more broken homes, fewer male role models, more television and video, more computer games, less time for intellectually stimulating play – have a greater effect on boys than on girls. Experienced teachers in infant schools confirm the trend for boys to be arriving at full-time schooling less prepared to sit and concentrate, less motivated towards books, more pre-disposed to opting out of the educational process and into 'laddishness'.

No wonder that by the time these boys reach the secondary school, the teachers there feel a sense of helplessness in the face of societal forces beyond their control. One reaction is to shrug the shoulders and simply 'carry on teaching', sometimes believing that it is wrong to take special measures with pupils of one gender. There is a widely held and, I believe, misguided perception that equality of opportunity means similarity of provision.

Another reaction is to accept that nature is now establishing the role of the female as the dominant influence in society. It is almost as if our historical biological programming, with the male as the strong silent hunter and the female as the communicative nest-provider, has failed to respond quickly enough to the changes in society. We are in a post-agrarian and post-industrial society in which the very skills with which females seem to be, in general, more endowed are at a premium. It can be argued that the trend for females to become more pre-eminent in society is one which should be welcomed, as there might be a hope that the world would become a more sensitive and caring place if the influence of the brutish male were reduced.

A third reaction to the problems experienced by boys and young men is to try to do something about it, within both primary and secondary schools, but without doing anything in favour of the boys which would have a negative effect on the girls. This is the philosophy which underpins this book. The strategies which are advocated and exemplified here strike at the heart of the issue: the day-to-day relationship between teacher and pupil. The essential theme is that teachers must re-think the language they use when communicating with boys inside and outside the classroom. Too often teachers radiate, unwittingly, an assumption of low expectation. The language they use reinforces the latent hostility of the disaffected boy; careful attention to the guidance and exercises in this book may help to break a deeply ingrained habit.

A generation ago, teachers who had been used to teaching in grammar or secondary modern schools had to come to terms with teaching in the comprehensive all-ability classroom. They realised that their teaching materials and techniques had to be flexible and adapted to the ability level and needs of the individual. The realisation today is that alongside differentiation by ability level comes the need for differentiation by gender. What this means in effect is that teachers are becoming better practitioners because they are thinking more carefully about the individuals in front of them.

If schools are to make a difference, it is essential that the whole school community is aware of the issue and committed to improvement. Only if teachers at all levels in the school (not just the senior management) collaborate with pupils and parents will progress be made. This book emphasises in particular the need for the active involvement of pupils. Improvement cannot be imposed on pupils; it needs their understanding and participation. Many workers in this field have realised, as has the present author, that the pupils themselves bring valuable insights and their views must be sought and acted upon. Parents too have a crucial role to play. After all, children only spend 15% of their waking time in a school setting between 5 and 16 so what happens in their family context makes a huge difference to their life chances.

Many schools have devoted one or more of their in-service training days to the topic of the impact of gender on performance. These are proving to be fruitful because they provoke teachers to think more sensitively about their relationship with pupils, about the relevance and intrinsic interest of their teaching materials and about the way they manage the classroom. But one-off days must be followed up by the development of practical policies and sustained monitoring of the impact of any actions taken.

For primary schools, a key issue must be boys' difficulties with reading and higher order comprehension skills. The inability to read fluently is a major stumbling-block to further progress. This book tackles this matter in a realistic and practical way.

Once awareness has been raised, much can be achieved by school-based action research and comparison with other similar schools. An interesting way forward is to identify schools which 'buck the trend' and to see what it is they are doing which seems to influence the performance of boys. If a school consistently over a number of years achieves a better performance from the boys than the girls, we need to find out why. Is this a fluke? Is something wrong with the girls? Is something special being done? Collaborative locally-based research can perhaps help to provide solutions.

This book rightly focuses on the performance of teachers in the classroom. Others are studying the impact of school organisation. For example, many co-educational schools are now experimenting with single-sex grouping, usually for selected subjects, occasionally for all subjects in Key Stage 3. Although this cannot of itself be seen as a panacea, it is offering some interesting insights. Teachers are saying that it is easier to teach effectively when they have pupils of one gender only in the room. Heads and Deputies creating timetables must ensure that the appropriate teachers are allocated to the classes although that does not necessarily mean that large males must teach the boys' groups. Some of the most effective teaching of boys-only groups is being carried out by female teachers. The most interesting finding to emerge is that single-sex teaching appears to raise the performance levels of both boys *and* girls, with the result that the 'gap' still remains. If everybody is doing better, does the 'gap' matter?

Perhaps the biggest challenge for secondary schools lies in the realm of Personal and Social Education and in that ill-defined area of 'school ethos'. Can we use PSE lessons and assemblies to counteract the prevailing social image of 'men behaving badly' and to put across the idea that it is perfectly acceptable for a boy to be 'masculine', keen on sport, popular with his peers and still enjoy reading, music, schoolwork and helping others?

Two decades ago there was much positive educational action in favour of girls in order to overcome some of the limitations placed upon females by tradition and social convention. The recent success of girls is to be wholly welcomed and needs to be extended beyond education to the wider working world. The time is now right for similar concern to be shown about the male of the species and for positive action to be taken.

Peter Downes

Peter Downes is a former President of the Secondary Heads Association and co-author of a SHA publication *Can Boys do Better?*. As a Senior Research Associate at Homerton College, Cambridge, he has worked on a project to explore the difficulties boys have in learning foreign languages.

Preface

The fact that boys are failing in school is now widely acknowledged. The 1997 report *Can boys do better?* by the Secondary Heads Association noted that girls outperformed boys in both GCSE and 'A' level and that more than 80% of those excluded from school are boys. The following statistics are from the Department for Education and Employment:[1]

- In literacy around 10% more girls than boys achieve the expected level or above in Key Stages 1 and 2.
- At Key Stage 3 the gap between boys and girls achieving the expected level increases to 17%.
- In mathematics and science boys' and girls' achievements are broadly similar.
- In 2000 10% more girls than boys achieved 5 A*-C grades at GCSE.
- In 1998/1999 two thirds of pupils in special schools were boys.

Although the gender gap is considerably smaller than the inequalities of attainment associated with ethnic origin and social class background, by 1995 this gap was present within each ethnic group regardless of social class background.[2]

It has long been known that boys and girls mature at different rates, and since the 1960s this has been taken account of in exams such as the '11 Plus'. However, in the past boys caught up or overtook girls by the time they left school. Both girls' and boys' levels of attainment have risen substantially since 1965, but girls have improved more.[3]

> *The gender gap in performance in relation to five or more A*-C passes emerged at the end of the 1980s; within four years the position had changed from one of rough equality between the sexes to clear disparity.*
>
> Arnot, Gray, James, Rudduck (1998)

What can individual teachers do about this situation? This book sets out to find some practical answers to this pressing question.

The idea for the book was conceived when, observing a Year 5 class, I noticed that the teacher – a competent, experienced and caring woman – had a problem with boys, or rather, with a certain kind of boy. I watched her work with the girls – the clever and the less clever, the quiet ones and the noisy ones. She was calm and encouraging, she understood them and knew how to get the best out of them. I saw her work with the quiet boys and the conscientious boys: there was a good rapport, she seemed to like and respect them. But when it came to the other boys, the 'boyish' boys, the ones with lots of energy and a mischievous outlook on life, there seemed to be a problem. She was impatient and irritable, nagging and reactive. She had no empathy with their boisterous energy, it was unwelcome in the classroom and she tried to suppress it.

I had seen one of these boys in a local pantomime and after the lesson I told the teacher how well he had done, expecting her to be pleased that he was at least displaying talent outside school. I was wrong: my observation simply confirmed her view of him. 'I'm not surprised,' she said in an exasperated tone, 'he's such a show-off!'

On another occasion an experienced secondary school teacher invited me to observe him work with a particularly difficult Year 9 class. At the end of the lesson he regretted the fact that he had to give so much more attention to the boys than the girls; he felt the girls were getting a raw deal. In terms of time, I agreed, the boys were getting more of his attention than the girls, but had he considered the quality of the attention he was giving? His comments to girls had been brief, friendly and encouraging – very positive in fact. His comments to boys had been about poor behaviour, lack of concentration and insufficient work; almost all the attention they received had been negative. We discussed how he could change the balance, not from boys to girls, but from negative to positive.

My son was about six at this time and he seemed to be turning into a 'boyish' kind of a boy. What hope had he in our education system, I wondered, if these problems with boys were as common as I suspected?

I set out to find out what motivated boys in school; to interview boys, teachers and parents about their experiences of boys in school, and to observe and record the most effective ways to communicate with boys in a teaching situation. I then ran a series of workshops for teachers to test the ideas and draw on the experience of those attending. This book is the result of those observations, interviews, conversations and workshops. The ideas have been explored in workshops with over 300 teachers, and many examples of good practice I have included were given to me by those teachers. I interviewed 24 boys between eight and eighteen years old, using questions designed to test my propositions. The questions and the replies – 'What the boys said' – are used to illustrate points made throughout the book.

If boys, as the statistics show, are underachieving in comparison with girls, what practical steps can we take to remedy this? Firstly, we can clarify the genuine differences between boys and girls and try to understand how this affects them in the classroom; secondly, we can value boys for who they are and get to like the rumbustious qualities many of them have; thirdly, we can learn skills that bring out the best in boys at school.

This book aims to be a practical handbook for teachers that is easy to digest and apply, focusing on practice rather than theory. The references and bibliography provide pointers for those who would like to go into the subject in more depth. Many of the points I make are illustrated by stories and case studies; all these are based on actual events and situations.

Chapter 1 examines factors that may influence the achievement of boys in schools; and each of the following chapters explores a specific area, first covering ideas that will help understand boys and then giving practical communication techniques to assist in that area. Key points for teachers are identified and then each point is explored in detail with examples, case studies and boys' views. Each chapter concludes with a summary of points. Throughout the book there are 'Notebook' boxes containing questions and exercises that can be used to explore the ideas further.

The book's emphasis is on communication strategies that can be used to engage and motivate boys in the classroom. Analysing the effect of what we say and looking at alternatives gives us a wider repertoire to draw on – helping us, when the pressure is on, to avoid falling into old patterns that may simply lead to an escalation of bad behaviour. The methods outlined here take no extra teaching time, can readily be incorporated into lessons and will reduce time spent on discipline in the future. This enables everyone in the class to benefit from a more productive learning environment.

In attempting to give insights into what boys are like, why many find themselves disadvantaged at school and how to accommodate their needs in the classroom I have, of necessity, made generalisations about the differences between boys and girls, and often refer to boys' 'typical' behaviours. I am aware of the danger and limitations of such generalisations, since boys and girls present a whole spectrum of personalities and behaviours, and both can become disaffected with school. The fact that many children do not conform to typical male or female norms is to be welcomed and celebrated. Nevertheless, in order to understand and *value* the 'boy qualities' that have often been unwelcome in the classroom, I believe we need to identify these qualities, give them labels and analyse them. Paradoxically, it is through this process of labelling boys' characteristics and exploring what these mean that we free boys from the negative labels they are often given. The examples I use tend towards the boisterous boy, and I make no apology for that, since these are the boys many teachers find take up so much of their time and attention.

How to use this book

I suggest you read the book through once quickly to get the philosophy and principles behind it, then work on the skills one chapter at a time, giving yourself at least a week to apply new skills in the classroom before moving on to the next chapter. If possible work with a colleague or group of colleagues so that you can compare your 'notebook exercises' and exchange ideas and experiences. Feel free to adapt ideas and suggestions to individual circumstances and personalities.

A final word before we start: this book explores the nature of boys and how to view them and communicate with them in a way that brings out their best. However, whilst I have been working on it I have been asked if I have a similar understanding of girls in school, or of black students. Neither are areas I have researched and both deserve proper attention in their own right. Nevertheless, you will find much here that can be applied to any student, whatever their personality, gender or race: the ideas and communication skills explored here can be adapted to bring out the best in anyone.

Chapter 1
Boys Will Be Boys

A five-year-old boy came home from school one day and said to his mother: 'Girls are cleverer than boys'.
'Who told you that?' she asked, surprised.
'Amy did.'
'And what do you think?'
'I think she's right.'

From the 1960s onwards many people came to believe that girls and boys were the same in most respects and that 'equal opportunities' would equalise educational performance. The relative fall in boys' achievement since then means that we need to re-examine this belief.

When I was at school in the 60s and early 70s girls were encouraged to reject the constraints of society's previous expectations of women. Many of my generation believed that any differences in behaviour and achievement were simply due to social conditioning and sexual stereotyping. Ours was the generation that would show there was no difference between men and women; and we would break the cycle of social conditioning by bringing up our children, when we had them, in a way that avoided gender stereotypes.

But when we had our own children we found there were innate differences between boys and girls that we could not deny. There

the seven ages of
BOYHOOD

age eighteen

baby

age three

age fifteen

age six

age twelve

age nine

are many anecdotes about children whose parents attempted to treat their sons and daughters the same. Boys not allowed toy guns improvised with anything from Lego bricks to crusts of bread. A mother who had filled the playroom with cars and construction kits but no dolls, overheard one daughter saying to the other 'Here's the mummy car, here's the daddy car and here's the baby car'. Parents of a set of twins, determined to bring them up the same, reported the girl preferring the dolls house while the boy preferred the bow and arrows, and neither being able to persuade their sibling to join them in their chosen game for long; at four the girl enjoyed sitting and colouring in neatly, while the boy made large squirly shapes with a fat felt-tipped pen. My house looks out into the middle of a village and over the years it has fascinated me to watch children at leisure, the girls frequently strolling through the village in twos or threes chatting, the boys more often running, cycling, skating or skateboarding. Research in pre-school and infant settings also confirms the different orientations of boys and girls.[1]

Few people now dispute that there are differences between boys and girls or men and women; the debate is about what causes these differences and what the consequences are for policy-making. That debate is much broader than the focus of this particular book, which aims to develop communication strategies for teachers to use in motivating boys. Nonetheless, before we explore how to motivate boys in school, it is worthwhile examining certain factors that may be affecting their educational performance. In this chapter we will look at:

- **Biological factors**
- **Social factors**
- **Educational factors**

Biological factors

While the environment in which children are nurtured clearly affects the way they turn out, research into gender shows that there are significant physiological and behavioural differences between boys and girls from birth.[2]

— Baby girls in the first few hours of life are much more interested in people and faces, while baby boys are as happy if objects are dangled in front of them.
— On average girls say their first words and learn to speak in short sentences earlier than boys.
— Boys are more active than girls, moving faster and spending more time in motion; girls spend more time in communication.[3]
— Girls read earlier than boys and find it easier to cope with grammar, spelling and punctuation.
— Boys have better 'spatial ability' which gives them superior hand-eye coordination for ball games, enables them to visualise easily in three-dimensions and makes them better than girls at construction, map-reading and chess.

Hearing and sight also differ between boys and girls:

— Girls are more sensitive to noise than boys, have wider peripheral vision and can see better in the dark.
— Boys see better in bright light, have a greater sense of perspective and observe in a more focused way. A typical boy, therefore, would be less able to read the verbal and visual nuances in communication than a girl and may literally not see that a classroom is untidy when he walks in, or that there is litter on the playground.

One significant gender difference is that young boys tend to have growing spurts that affect their ear canals. The ear canal stretches, thins and often blocks up, leading to periods of hearing loss. A boy often 'cops it' at school or home for not listening, not doing what he is told. The problem may affect one boy in class this month and another boy a month later. It's temporary, and it just means you have to make sure boys hear what you are saying to them. Sometimes they are not naughty, just deaf!
Steve Biddulph, *Raising Boys*

Many differences between boys and girls can be explained through differences between the typical male and female brain. Higher thought processes take place in the cortex, the layer covering both halves of the brain, but these functions occupy different parts of the cortex in boys and girls. Female brains also have more connections between the hemispheres than in the male brain. The table below looks at four functions in typical male and female brains that have a bearing on performance at school.

Function	Location in Males	Location in Females
Mechanics of language	left hemisphere front & back	left hemisphere front
Vocabulary	left hemisphere front & back	left & right hemisphere front & back
Visio-spatial perception	right hemisphere	right & left hemisphere
Emotion	right hemisphere	right & left hemisphere

Such research shows that the male brain is more specialised, with each of these four crucial functions being located in just one hemisphere, whilst in females three of the functions take place in *both* hemispheres.[4]

The make-up of the male brain may explain the difficulty boys often have in expressing their emotions. Girls' emotional and verbal brain functions are in both hemispheres, while these are in separate hemispheres in boys. A boy therefore has fewer connections between the hemispheres than a girl, making it harder for information about the emotions to flow to the verbal function and hence more difficult for him to express what he is feeling. A girl can think and feel at the same time whereas a boy tends to do one or the other.

Research has shown that more connections between the hemispheres makes a person more articulate and fluent, which may further explain girls' verbal dexterity.

In the early school years, children concentrate on reading and writing, skills that largely favour girls. As a result, boys fill remedial reading classes, don't learn to spell, and are classified as dyslexic or learning-disabled four times as often as girls. Had these punitive categories existed earlier they would have included Faraday, Edison and Einstein.
Dianne McGuinness, *When Children Don't Learn*

One of the main reasons girls and boys perform differently at school is that differences in physiology predispose them to be more able in certain areas than others. Schools must recognise both sets of characteristics and play to both sets of strengths, so that all pupils are able to thrive in the school environment.

Testosterone

Another key physiological difference between boys and girls is the balance of hormones affecting their bodies. Hormone levels vary between individuals, and the description overleaf gives an idea of what happens to a typical boy or girl.

In the first weeks of pregnancy there is no noticeable difference between a male and female embryo. At around the sixth week testosterone starts to be made in the male embryo. This stimulates the development of the male sexual organs, lays down the blue-print for how the neural pathways will be laid out and programmes the brain to respond to increases in testosterone levels later in life.

Once the testicles are formed they produce additional testosterone and by the time the baby is born he has as much testosterone flowing around his body as a twelve-year-old boy. A few months after birth the testosterone levels in boys fall away and remain similar to that of girls throughout babyhood and toddlerhood.

At the age of four boys receive their next surge of testosterone and tend to become more interested in action, adventure and vigorous play. At five testosterone levels drop again and the hormone levels in boys and girls are roughly equivalent for a few years. At eight the female hormone levels start to rise in girls, they become more rounded, start to develop breasts and at around thirteen begin their menstrual cycle.

Boys' testosterone levels rise sharply between eleven and thirteen, causing sudden growth that requires some 'rewiring' of the nervous system to keep pace with these changes. As a result of the building programme taking place in his body, a boy can become temporarily disorganised and dopey during these years.[5]

Testosterone levels reach their peak in boys at around fourteen. This increases body muscle, prompts the voice to break and generates strong sexual feelings, general restlessness and a desire to test limits. It also affects the way the brain functions: IQ tests show that between fourteen and sixteen boys catch up with girls on written and verbal ability and surge ahead in mathematical ability, though whether this ability is realised probably depends on other factors.

Research into both humans and animals show that testosterone produces the following characteristics: energetic and boisterous behaviour, competition and need for hierarchy, self-confidence and self-reliance, risk-taking and single-mindedness. **These characteristics, which will be displayed in many boys at school, need to be recognised, valued and managed.**

Boys have always been interested in adventure and mischief, though each generation of adults has a habit of forgetting this. Mark Twain reminds us in his preface to 'The Adventures of Tom Sawyer':

Most of the adventures recorded in this book really occurred. Huck Finn is drawn from life; Tom Sawyer also...he is the composition of three boys I knew. ... Part of my plan has been to pleasantly remind adults of what they once were themselves, and of how they felt and thought and talked, and what queer enterprises they sometimes engaged in.

Males tend to be more assertive and also more aggressive than females, and testosterone levels rise after aggressive behaviour. Boys may need to be tutored in ways to manage their aggression and find appropriate outlets for it. Australian parenting expert Steve Biddulph has coined the term TNT (Testosterone Needing

Tuition). He compares it to PMT (Pre-Menstrual Tension) and suggests that, just as a good husband understands his partner's PMT, so the adults in a boy's life need to understand his TNT.[6]

Social factors

The social changes that took place in the latter half of the twentieth century have left men with an ambiguous role in society. Previously delineations had been clear: girls expected to become mothers and homemakers while boys expected to become fathers and breadwinners, protecting their family or country as and when necessary. They would join a trade or profession in which they anticipated staying – a job for life. Several changes took place that altered much of that:

- The spread of mechanisation and decline in jobs requiring manual labour
- The increase in jobs requiring communication and social skills
- Fewer industries providing jobs for life
- Feminism which led to women re-defining themselves as more than homemakers
- The growth in one-parent families with children usually raised by the mother

The change in the way society views women has resulted in many girls becoming more confident, recognising that they have choices and can take control of their life. This confidence is encouraged by the media, particularly television, where women and girls are often portrayed as clever, strong and capable, taking on previously male roles of 'fighter' or 'leader'. This trend would be excellent if it were not for the simultaneous tendency, recently, to highlight women's abilities at the expense of men. In many TV adverts you will find men portrayed as trying but failing, the butt of the joke or simply inadequate. The theme is 'Superwoman' gets one over on 'Mr Nice-but-Useless'. Even (or especially) the 'new man' who is doing the housework cannot get it right and is made fun of for not being as competent as his partner. Not surprisingly there has been a backlash – programmes like 'Men Behaving Badly' and the rise of 'laddism', a masculinity defined by males for males.

> The departure lounge is full of tourists awaiting a charter flight after a fortnight's holiday in the Mediterranean. There is a delay. The children rush around the lounge, returning to their parents from time to time. A twelve-year-old girl starts chasing a ten-year-old boy. Carla is strong and confident. Matthew, of average build for his age, is smaller, less strong and rather flattered by her attentions. The chase ends in a play fight. Carla floors Matthew and pins him to the ground, he admits defeat and returns to his mother to lick some of his wounds. Carla struts around; pleased with her victory, she comes within earshot and crows:
>
> 'Girls rule, boys drool!'

Whilst boys' perceptions of masculinity may be heavily influenced by society, the strongest influence comes from the home. Mothers provide a role model for their daughters, but they also provide their sons and daughters with many lessons on the nature of men. If children see a respectful, loving relationship and hear their mother talking about their father and other men with affection and respect, they take on these attitudes. If their mother puts their father down the children may learn to despise their father in particular and men in general. This causes obvious difficulties for a boy since he will, one day, become a man himself and hence someone to be despised. The difficulties increase if he has no male role model to draw on.

The father is a key role model for boys, as they will learn from him more than from anyone else what it means to be male. The roles on offer seem to be polarising and diverging: the 'New Father' who is highly involved with his family, the 'Absent Father' who, due to divorce or work commitments (the British work longer hours than any other country in Europe) is not available to his children, and the 'Macho Father' who uses verbal or physical aggression to rule the roost. A survey of 1400 British boys[7] found that the involvement of a father or father figure had a significant affect on boys' self-esteem and their attitude to school. Boys with a man in their life who spends time with them, does activities with them, listens to their problems and gives them guidance are most likely to have high self-esteem and a positive outlook toward school. Interestingly, *the level of involvement* of the father figure was more important than whether or not he lived with the boy.

In the absence of good male role models in the family, boys may look elsewhere to find a model for masculinity. If they do not find suitable role models in other adults they will look to other young men to find out what maleness should be. In the confusion commonly experienced around masculinity, boys' tendency is to define 'boy' as 'not girl' and to include attributes such as 'coolness', 'hardness', sporting prowess, an anti-work ethic and homophobia.[8]

> *Men in positions of contact with boys, whether teachers or youth workers or sports coaches, should be more aware of the strength of their responsibility and influence as sign-posts on the path from boy to man.*
>
> Adrienne Katz, *Leading Lads*

Educational factors

In Britain children start full-time schooling when they are four and a half or five years old. Many European countries wait until children are six or seven before they start formal schooling and by the time they are 11 their reading levels are on a par with British children. It is boys who particularly suffer from this early start. There is some evidence that in countries where children start school later and have good early years education before beginning compulsory school, the gender gap at age nine is almost negligible, while earlier compulsory schooling leads to a greater gender gap.[9]

At five a boy is typically less able to be still, to concentrate, to listen or to communicate than a girl and has a greater need for variety, stimulation and physical activity.

Girls tend to be dextrous and have good 'on-the-table skills'. Their attributes are valued and praised and many settle into school well. Boy attributes are less welcome, their energy and lack of concentration is often interpreted as bad behaviour or lack of application and they are frequently told off. Many decide at an early age that school is not for them – a place to be endured rather than enjoyed.

A combination of recent education policies has increased the pressure for children to be introduced to the school environment even earlier.[10] Some schools are asking parents of children as young as three to register to ensure a place, and many parents believe that they are more likely to get a place if their child attends the school nursery. This puts boys who are not ready for nursery at a further disadvantage.

When my son started school he went half time and each day returned happy and enthusiastic, impressed at the range of construction kits, and enjoying new friends. After half term he went full time. At the end of the first week he announced that he didn't want to go to school all day and would come home in the afternoon again: he was unaware that there was no real choice. By the third week, he seemed to realise that school was for life, the enthusiasm went and an air of resignation came over him. I described this experience to a head teacher and he recognised it at once. Every year, he said, he observed the lights going out in the eyes of some five-year-old boys. An experienced classroom assistant told me that it was usual for reception children to go down with a cold soon after their first half term. She put it down to lots of children and November germs. Perhaps. Or could it be a psychosomatic response to school?

Other well-intentioned policies have had negative ramifications for boys. Since the 1980s, assessment at GCSE and 'A' Level has moved from being primarily exam-based to incorporating increased amounts of coursework. Exams require short bursts of intense effort, the retention of information (if only for a short time), quality of thought rather than quantity of writing and speed rather than neatness. These demands favour typical male attributes. Coursework, on the other hand, requires sustained effort over a period of time, records of process as well as outcome, and a large amount of well-presented written work – all of which favour typical female attributes.

The wizard's first rule

In Terry Goodkind's fantasy novel 'Wizard's First Rule' novice wizards are cautioned that those who attempt to do good often end up inadvertently doing harm. Policymakers could do well to take note of this.[11]

Concerns about standards in education have led to the introduction of the National Curriculum and Standard Attainment Testing (SATS). These have emphasized academic attainment for every age group, often at the expense of practical activities, which many, especially younger children, prefer. As we have seen, while girls can generally adapt to these demands, boys may find this much harder. The publication of league tables and publicity of OFSTED inspection results puts teachers (and children) under immense pressure to 'perform'. In many cases this spotlight leads to conservative teaching methods, such as 'teaching to the test', rather than using imagination and inspiration to motivate children to learn. Many girls survive the experience with few ill effects; but a lot of boys switch off education all together, some before they leave primary school. It is ironic that tools successive governments have introduced to raise standards may be part of the cause of boys' underachievement.

Another factor that may have a detrimental effect on the performance of boys is the increase in the proportion of female teachers. This has three effects: firstly, it has left boys with fewer male role models (it is not uncommon to find primary schools with no male staff at all); secondly, boys may conclude that learning is a female activity and hence not something relevant to them; and thirdly, the shift has moved schools towards female norms and values – 'feminine' qualities such as order and conscientiousness are valued, while 'masculine' qualities of energy, humour and daring can be perceived as disruptive.

Summary and conclusion

This chapter has explored some of the reasons underlying the current underachievement of boys in school. Understanding is a crucial first step, since it is not until the needs of boys are understood that these can be met. **A large part of the problem for boys is that they are perceived (and dealt with) as a problem.**

There seem to be three factors that account for the differences in the behaviour and performance of boys and girls in school: biological, educational and social. Equal opportunities have emphasised sameness, but biological factors need to be understood so that differences can be appreciated and catered for. Education in Britain has changed considerably since the 1980s, not least with its emphasis on targets, inspection and standards. Social factors have a great influence on how children perceive themselves and on the choices they make. Recent changes in the patterns of family and work leave many asking 'What is a man supposed to be in the 21st Century?' Many boys are confused by the conflicting messages they receive and, having no clear adult models, look to their peers for a definition of masculinity.

When teachers recognise the difficulties boys face in the early 21st Century, they can help them define 'boy' in a productive way and show boys and girls how to recognise their strengths and value their differences.

Changes in education, the family and employment have empowered many women and girls. Sadly, some of this has been at the expense of boys and men. As we embark on the project of empowering boys, let's not make this mistake again, but instead empower both genders simultaneously.[12]

> *It became apparent that simply talking about experiences helped many boys to consider what alternative ways of 'doing boy' could be available to them.*
>
> Frosh, Phoenix & Pattman, *Young Masculinities*

I was once asked to run a series of Equal Opportunities courses for managers. In trying to get to grips with the nub of what equal opportunities entailed, I realised that practising equal opportunities was actually practising good management – attempting to bring out the best in each person who worked for you. In the same way, practising equal opportunities in schools means using effective teaching methods to bring out the best in each child you teach. Some techniques to achieve this are explored in the chapters that follow.

A primary head teacher, wanting to improve the self-esteem of the boys in her school, decided to do an assembly on 'Discoveries and Inventions'. She told the children of the many discoveries and inventions that allowed them to enjoy the quality of life they did. And, she added, almost all of these were discovered or invented by men. Men and boys have an interesting way of thinking, she explained, a creative mind, and many of the world's geniuses were men. She watched the boys' reaction to this information: slumped postures straightened, chests puffed out and faces lit up with pride. They had a new view of themselves and their potential.

Chapter 2

Valuing Boys For Who They Are

Treat people as if they were what they ought to be and you help them to become what they are capable of being.

Goethe

Boys' characteristics

The way boys often behave is beautifully described by child psychologists Dan Kindlon and Michael Thompson in their book 'Raising Cain':[1]

> Boys generally are an active lot, and often impulsive. Their energy is contagious, especially among other boys, and that physical energy can translate into a kind of psychological boldness. They often are the risk takers, seemingly oblivious to the potential hurt of a fall or sting of reprimand. Whether their choices might eventually prove to be brave or reckless, boys are often in the middle of an action before they consider the consequences.

> Boys are direct; they act in simple terms ... Emotional immaturity allows them to celebrate themselves unabashedly, strutting, boasting, clamouring to be noticed. They're not terribly concerned about pleasing others ... Boys' need to feel competent and empowered leads them to express a keen, power-based, action-oriented sense of justice, fairness, good and evil.

These qualities serve boys beautifully in the playground. In the classroom ... 'boy qualities' quickly turn from assets to liabilities.

To paraphrase Kindlon and Thompson, boys are typically:

— energetic
— action-orientated
— physical

A boy with no outlet for his energy may feel trapped. Some boys respond by switching off, appearing well-behaved when in fact they have withdrawn; others bring their energy into the classroom on their own terms through horseplay, shouting out and pushing things to the limit. A teacher's challenge is to tap into boys' energy rather than suppressing it, then channel the energy into creative tasks.

Why God Made Boys

God made a world out of his dreams
Of magic mountains, oceans and streams,
Prairies and plains and wooded land,
Then paused and thought, 'I need someone
To stand on top of the mountains, to conquer the sea,
Explore the plains and climb the trees,
Someone to start out small and grow
Sturdy, strong like a tree', and so
He created boys, full of spirit and fun
To explore and conquer, to romp and run,
With dirty faces, banged up chins,
With courageous hearts and boyish grins.
When he had completed the task he'd begun,
He surely said, 'That's a job well done'.

Cathy Craft, Classroom Assistant

It seems to me that boys particularly value:

— excitement
— humour
— courage
— justice

Most boys seek out excitement, whether by thinking up an adventurous game or story, speeding about on their bike/skates/ motorbike, exploring places where they are not permitted to go, pushing boundaries to the limit, or losing themselves in a Playstation adventure.

> Of the 24 boys interviewed, 12 used words 'boring', 'bored' or 'the same each day' to describe school.

Humour also plays an important part in many boys' lives:

'We like messing around, we laugh at everything.'   Christian, 12

Boys like to take risks and seem to recognise and value courage in their own and others' actions: a boy who rides his BMX off a high ramp or tells a teacher what he thinks of her may be seen as brave by his peers rather than foolhardy or rude. Teachers report that boys have a particularly keen sense of justice, based on their own (sometimes quite complex) sets of rules.

> Of the 24 boys interviewed, 13 reported that perceived injustices made them feel angry at school.

A boy who finds nothing exciting or humorous in his school day will become bored and mischievous, then create his own excitement and humour, probably not to his teachers' liking; if he experiences injustice he may be brave enough to rebel. But if teachers make a point of bringing the qualities that boys value into the classroom, this will motivate many of the boys they teach. How to do so will be covered later in the book.

Most people, including boys, want to be:

- accepted
- respected
- admired

To what extent do we accept, respect and admire our boys? As a society, I suggest, we are not doing too well, as the following story suggests.

An eleven-year-old boy took a walk by the canal. He soon found some attractive stones to put in his pocket and a long stick to walk with. He seldom came back from a walk without an interesting stone or a good shaped stick, though sometimes he would settle for a fir cone instead. He spotted some ducks on the path. He crept up to them quietly, seeing how close he could get without frightening them. There was a loud yell from the other side of the canal. The boy started. 'Stop harassing the ducks!' a woman shouted from a moored narrow boat, 'Get away from them!'

The boy, feeling sullen, for he loved animals and had enjoyed being so close, moved on. The woman watched with hands on hips until she was confident of the safety of the ducks. Once the boy had left, a fisherman arrived with his four-year-old daughter. As the man set up his fishing gear the child played. She spotted the ducks and went towards them, trying to get as close as she could. The woman noted the scene – the fisherman, the little girl and the ducks – and, smiling contentedly, went back into the narrow boat cabin.

The extent to which individual schools and teachers accept, respect and admire their boys will vary considerably, but it is possible that the teaching profession reflects this aspect of society more than we might wish.

> *The teachers who respect you are polite and courteous. If you get a question wrong they say 'Unlucky' or 'Try again'. Teachers say we've got to be nice to them, but they can be terrible to us. If you respect a teacher they should respect you. I didn't feel at all respected at school.*
>
> David, 16

A boy who feels neither accepted nor respected may become rebellious or disrespectful and will look to his peers to fulfil his needs. If he does not get the admiration he yearns for from his teachers, he will seek it from fellow-students, both boys and girls: admiration for his humour, for acting cool or for breaking the rules.

A boy who feels valued and respected will soften and show you his best side. Simply making the decision to see the best in the boys in your class will create a positive change in them. Using language to demonstrate that you value them for who they are will amplify that change. The rest of this chapter explores how to convey to boys that they are valued, and what to say to them so that they get this message loud and clear.

How to let boys know they are valued

- Acknowledge a boy's view of the world
- Convey respect in your words, body language and tone of voice
- Show admiration for their positive qualities

nowledge a boy's view of the world

The experience of many boys is that no one really listens to them and that adults are more interested in controlling them than finding out who they are and what they have to say. An effective way to show that you accept and respect someone is to listen to them and acknowledge what they say – without comment, judgment or opinion. Acknowledgment does not imply agreement or approval; it simply demonstrates a desire to understand the other. If a boy feels really heard and understood by a teacher he is likely to give respect and co-operation in return.

Acknowledgment needs only a sincere word or two. It is often true that the less a teacher says, the more a boy opens up and draws his own intelligent conclusions. The example below shows how a few words of acknowledgment allowed a seven-year-old boy to sort out a playground fight without the teacher needing to take any disciplinary action.

Example

Boy: 'Sam hit me in the playground!'
Teacher: *'I see.'*
Boy: 'I was showing him the karate moves I learnt last week and he suddenly hit me!'
Teacher: *'Oh!'*
Boy: 'Maybe he thought I was going to hit him.'
Teacher: *'Mmmm.'*
Boy: 'I'll go and tell him that I was only showing him how we do it and I'm not going to kick or punch him.
Teacher: *'Right.'*

People make many judgments about boys and their interests: they are immature, obsessed with fighting, computer-mad, sport-crazy, macho. Even the word puerile (boy-like) is pejorative. While a teacher may not relate to or agree with a boy's view of the world, it is important that he or she acknowledges that view as real. This allows the boy to experience his own validity. The examples below show how a teacher can acknowledge a boy's-eye view.

Example

The teacher knows that the majority of the boys in the school support a particular Premier Division football club who lost badly the evening before. She notices at the beginning of the first lesson that the boys are subdued and glum, and says:

'I hear Arsenal lost the match last night; did any of you watch it?'
There are affirmative groans around the room. *'I can see you are pretty cheesed off by the result.'*

The teacher cannot change the result of the match, but at least she has some idea about how they are feeling today and why, has shown some empathy and can adapt the lesson to take account of the mood of the class.

Example

In a Maths lesson Steven was struggling and wailed to his teacher, 'It's all gone out of my head!' The simplest way to acknowledge a boy's view of the world is to acknowledge what he says.

'It's all gone out of your head, Steven. Let's see if we can get some of it back.'

Example

At break time a teacher saw two eight year old boys hiding around the side of a building looking as if they were about to jump out on a friend. They were out of bounds. The teacher approached them with a smile and said:

'You two look like you're going to give your friend a big surprise, but actually you aren't supposed to be here. Why don't you go and hide over there?' The boys ran off grinning, planning their next surprise.

Example

A teacher came out of school to see three fifteen year olds on their BMX bikes; they were not in any of the classes she taught. One had been jumping over a milk bottle and left it rolling on the pavement as they rode off.

'Excuse me,' the teacher called. On the second call the boy stopped and turned round. *'You seem to be having a good time on that bike,'* she said, *'I'm worried someone will trip over the milk bottle. Can you put it back where you found it?'* 'I'm sorry!' responded the boy and returned the milk bottle to the doorstep.

A boy's natural curiosity is often misinterpreted by teachers: my husband remembers a science lesson on temperature when he was rebuked for taking the temperature of ink; a ten year old I interviewed who asked his Geography teacher how mountains were made, was told to stop asking silly questions. The teacher sees or hears non-conformism and, rather than recognising a search for knowledge, interprets it as disruption. In these cases, healthy inquisitiveness should be recognised and admired, while the boy's timing can be managed:

Instead of: 'Stop playing with that ink and get back to work.'

say: *'It's good to see you using your initiative in this investigation, but I'd like you to stick to the materials in the list for now.'*

Instead of: 'Stop asking silly questions.'

say: *'You'd like to know how mountains are made, Jordan. That's an interesting question and we will be covering it in Geography next year. But if you can't wait that long, come and find me at lunchtime and I'll lend you some books about it.'*

NOTEBOOK

Select a day when you will concentrate on acknowledging boys and the world they inhabit. During that day use acknowledgment to demonstrate an appreciation of where boys are coming from. Acknowledge individual boys, groups of boys and the class as a whole. Record in your notebook any differences in your response to boys' behaviour, or their response to you.

One way to get an angle on where boys are coming from is to ask them.

CASE STUDY

The after-school five-a-side football club has become a victim of its own success and lots of boys between eleven and sixteen turn up after school for a game. They have loads of energy to burn off: off the pitch this converts to noise, jostling, competitive posturing between rivals, and bigger boys chasing and pinning down smaller ones; on the pitch it becomes rough play and little consideration for others. The teacher has to referee very tightly to keep a lid on the game and can no longer trust those waiting their turn to behave. All his energy and attention is used to keep control and he realises he no longer enjoys running the club.

While on duty at lunchtime he decides to ask the opinions of some of the boys involved. The older ones say that they would like to play for longer and don't like all the waiting around. The younger ones say the older ones are too rough and recommend splitting the club by age, maybe on different afternoons. The teacher mulls this over: yesterday he was considering closing the club and, to his surprise, today he is considering doing two sessions a week.

In the event, he changes from one hour-and-a-half session to two one-hour sessions for different age groups. The boys are calmer and more responsible, the teacher is able to concentrate on improving skill levels rather than crowd control and he finds his previous enthusiasm for the club has returned.

In many situations it would be unhelpful for a teacher to get into a discussion with pupils about why or how things should be done – they simply need to be done. In some instances, however, potentially confrontational situations can be avoided by asking a boy to explain his point of view, as shown in the examples below.

Example

A boy who repeatedly breaks a rule might be taken aside and asked: *'Is there anything about this rule you don't understand or don't agree with?'* This will only work if your voice demonstrates you are genuinely interested in his point of view; if there is any hint of sarcasm this will backfire. It is important to listen to his reply and acknowledge his point of view, though this does not mean you have to agree with it.

Example

If a boy often gets angry when he is punished and you suspect he has felt unfairly treated in the past, you might, after giving him a sanction, say: *'Do you think I dealt with that fairly?'* Sometimes pupils say 'yes' because they think they are supposed to. If you think that is the case you could say: *'You don't sound as though you do. Is there anything that seems unfair to you?'*

Another situation: a frequently unmotivated boy is showing little interest in the project work he has been asked to do. When the teacher asks if there's a problem the boy says it's boring.

Instead of: 'It's only boring because you are making it boring.'
ask: *'What makes it boring – too hard / too easy / too much writing / you aren't interested in the subject?'*

(If you ask a boy why something is boring without giving him some options he may not be able to give you a useful reply.)

CASE STUDY

Faber and Mazlish[2] describe the approach a school Principal used when fighting students were sent to him. He would sit them at either end of his desk and ask them to write a report on what had happened. Before writing anything they would invariably make an assertion like: 'It was his fault!' or 'He started it!'

'Write that down,' the Principal replied, 'Don't leave anything out.' Once the reports had been written the Principal would read them out, acknowledging each student's point of view. He then asked for their recommendations; and once an agreement had been reached, allowed them to return to class.

Some teachers are concerned that they do not have enough time to acknowledge individual boys, and that doing so is just another way of giving them more than their fair share of attention. But if a pupil is taking up your attention anyway, to acknowledge where he is coming from is unlikely to take additional time; if he then feels recognised and accepted for who he is, he is more likely to cooperate in class, saving time in the long run.

CASE STUDY

A few weeks after running a training day for a primary school I phoned the head teacher.

'I always thought I was good at this stuff,' she said, 'but after your course I've been watching what boys do in a completely different way. They've been making a mud pit in the playground. As a woman I can't relate to it and my first reaction is "It's

messy, so they shouldn't do it." But actually they aren't doing any harm, it completely absorbs their attention, and they're probably learning a lot too. In fact, I'm thinking of building a wallow hole for them.'

Acknowledging someone's reality can be difficult when you think it is wrong, but it can save a lot of disagreement.

Example

Six-year-old Jason comes onto the carpet, pushes Jane from where she was sitting, and plonks himself down there. Jane objects loudly and tells the teacher. Jason insists it was his place. As far as the teacher is concerned there is no such thing as 'my place' on the carpet.

Instead of: 'Don't be silly Jason, Jane was not sitting in your place.'
(Oh yes she was!)

say: *'I understand that Jane was sitting where you wanted to sit, Jason, but if you want something in this class, you ask, you do not push or hurt people.'*

By moving in the boy's direction you make it easier for him to come towards you in response.

Example

The Year 6 boys seemed to be obsessed with wrestling moves from WWF (World Wrestling Federation) and despite a no fighting rule frequently tried out the latest wrestling moves on each another in the playground. After his initial revulsion at the aggressiveness of the boys, their teacher decided to try and understand their fascination and asked them to tell him all about WWF. They enthusiastically told him the names of their favourite wrestlers, described the different moves, and explained how all the fights were choreographed and rehearsed to make them as entertaining as possible while reducing the danger to the participants. The teacher listened with interest, pointed out that hurting one another was exactly what he was concerned about, and asked which moves they used on each other and what damage they could do. They came up with several potentially serious injuries.

'I think you are right,' said the teacher, 'and with potential injuries like that you can see why I can't let you practise WWF in the playground. But I'm really impressed with what you know about it and I'd like to put up a display. Draw me some pictures at home of the wrestlers and the moves you described, and for each move write its advantages and potential hazards.'

Over the next few days the boys brought in pictures for the display and when it was complete the teacher got them to explain it in class and take questions. They were animated, informative and enthusiastic.

Convey respect in your words, body language and tone of voice

In their hearts most teachers respect their pupils. However, at the end of a stressful day when a pupil has done something really irritating, your facial expression, tone of voice and body language may not demonstrate that respect. Unfortunately, boys do not know what is in our hearts, but draw conclusions from what they see and hear. Overbearing body language, a harsh tone of voice, poorly chosen language and an unwillingness to listen can all convey disrespect.

The teachers I feel respected by value what you say or anything you suggest. They accept that you can get it wrong

Mike, 18

Respect is a two-way thing. Teachers that get respect talk to students, not down to them. They understand my view of their subject, and might say 'Look, I know you don't like Maths...'

James, 16

It is important to be aware of facial expressions, body language and your tone of voice. They should usually demonstrate firmness, warmth and care and always convey respect.

Example

> A supply teacher noticed two boys whispering while she was talking to the class. She had noticed earlier that one of the boys seemed to have great difficulty concentrating. She looked at the two kindly and, with warmth in her voice, firmly said:
>
> *'Your conversation looks like it's really interesting, but right now I'd like you to listen to what I'm saying.'* Both boys paid attention for the next ten minutes.

Most people react badly if they feel patronised or humiliated, but boys often become more obviously rebellious. Boys often complain that when they ask for help they are treated as though they are 'thick', and everything is re-explained in long and unnecessary detail. Because the teacher's tone of voice seems patronising to the boy, he switches off. Thus we have a self-fulfilling prophecy – the teacher treats the boy as stupid and the boy reacts by appearing stupid – and this is the start of a downward cycle of learning. The Topman survey of boys[3] identified and compared groups of boys who were 'pro-school' and 'anti-school':

Twice as many anti-school people report that it is 'very true' that they 'are made to feel stupid if you make a mistake' (28% vs. 13%). To protect his pride many a lad would rather 'muck about' than be seen as a fool.

Adrienne Katz, *Leading Lads*

When teachers tell boys off, their tone of voice often conveys anger, frustration, disrespect or dislike. Instead of listening to the words being said, boys react to the tone of voice. If you want them to listen to a rebuke, then your voice should sound firm and committed, but must not contain any additional emotional

NOTEBOOK

Try saying these sentences at different volumes and in different tones of voice, some as though to an individual, and some as though to a class. Ask a colleague whether you sound firm and respectful. Does your tone of voice, facial expression or body language convey any additional messages?

- Don't interrupt me whilst I am talking.
- See me at the end of the lesson.
- Listen to what I am saying.
- Where are you going?
- You don't understand this part.
- I don't want to have to tell you again.
- Be quiet.
- When the classroom is tidy you may go.
- I heard that.
- I'm getting very irritated.

You may have noticed that none of these sentences include the words 'please' or 'thank you'. This is so you can be sure that your *tone of voice on its own* conveys the respect, without relying on social conventions to compensate.

Make a note of any situations where your tone or body language might seem disrespectful and think of ways you can adjust your tone and body language to convey respect.

messages. This will allow them to hear the *content* of your message rather than react to the tone by switching off or retaliating.

Show admiration for boys' positive qualities

If boys want admiration, where will they seek it? Initially from everyone: their mothers and fathers, their siblings and friends, teachers and classmates, relations and neighbours. If they fail to get it in one place, they will simply look for it in another. So the boy who wants the admiration of his father, but fails to get it, may hope for admiration from his male teachers. He wants to be recognised as a 'young man' and will choose his role models from those who recognise him as such. If he gets no admiration from the men in his life, then he will look solely to his peers. But the qualities they admire (and hence encourage) may not be qualities adults find admirable.

> *I like to get told off because I like to impress the hard lot and it stops them calling me a boffin.*   Carl, 15

A boy also wants to be admired by the females in his life. And if women do not recognise his wit, dress-sense, courage, ability at sport or his sensitivity and ability to listen, then no doubt some of the girls will. Have you noticed how even the 'nicest' girls can be enthralled by boys' outrageous stories or off-the-wall behaviour? Teachers can encourage boys by looking out for things to admire.

Examples

- *'Nice haircut, Tim.'*

- *'Come on Jack, show us how it's done!'*

- *'Nearly finished, Joshua? Good man!'*

- *'You do make me laugh, James, but we are going to have to work on your timing!'*

- *'We've heard a lot from Lewis, Alex and James. Now I want to hear from Kirsten, Sharnie and Fay.'*

- *'You certainly know your way round a computer. '*

- *'That was chaos to order in three minutes, class, most impressive!'*

Teachers can also demonstrate admiration for qualities that boys have not yet learned to value.

Examples

- *'I was really impressed to see you working on that for so long.'*

- *'I noticed the way you held back and let others participate.'*

- *'By being honest about how you felt about this topic, you allowed others to share their true thoughts too – that really helped the discussion.'*

- *'When I asked for ten minutes silence, I wasn't sure you'd make it. You've exceeded my expectations!'*

Birthday cards are a great opportunity to acknowledge what you admire in your pupils, and allow you to focus your attention on one pupil at a time over the year. If you send them to their home address there is no opportunity for comparison or teasing, the boy's parents will see your message and the boy will probably put it in his 'treasure place' and keep it all year.

HAPPY BIRTHDAY
to someone with loads of energy,
boundless imagination
and a wonderful smile

HAPPY BIRTHDAY
to the boy I rely on when
the computer goes wrong!

HAPPY BIRTHDAY
Thanks for looking after
the rabbit all term.

HAPPY BIRTHDAY
Welcome to the class.
I'm looking forward to getting to know you.

NOTEBOOK

Jot down a few things you admire about the boys you teach and how you could express this in an appropriate way.

Conclusion

In his *Seven Habits of Highly Effective People* Stephen Covey refers to the emotional bank account. This is a metaphor to describe trust in a relationship. He tells how deposits are made through courtesy, kindness, honesty and keeping commitments, whilst withdrawals are made by discourtesy, disrespect, lack of attention and breaking agreements. When things get difficult, there is most give and take when the emotional bank account has a lot in reserve. If the account is low there is little room for manoeuvre. A boy who experiences acceptance, respect and admiration from his teachers is likely to have a healthy emotional bank balance, and troubled times will be easier because he is more likely to give you credit.

Chapter summary

Showing boys they are valued

Acknowledge their view of the world

♦ Try to see the world through the eyes of a boy
♦ Empathise with boys' thoughts and feelings
♦ Acknowledge their point of view, even when you don't agree with it

Convey respect in your words, body language and tone

♦ Be aware of your voice and your body language
♦ Treat each boy as a person, not a 'pain'
♦ Avoid sounding patronising when boys ask for help
♦ Let your words rebuke, not your tone of voice

Show admiration for their positive qualities

♦ Find admirable qualities in the boys you teach
♦ Tell them what you admire
♦ Show admiration for qualities they haven't yet learned to value

Chapter 3

Allowing Boys To Be Their Best

Children who behave badly in school are those whose self-esteem is threatened by failure. They see academic work as 'unwinnable'. They soon realise that the way to avoid losing such a competition is not to enter it.

The Elton Report

Freeing boys from labels

When doing the research for this book I asked an infant teacher of thirty years experience to tell me what she knew about boys. 'Well,' she replied, 'There are two sorts of boys – thugs and wimps.'

I was surprised at these stark stereotypes, but testing them out on others, many recognised the categories. The trouble with labels like 'thug' and 'wimp' is that they only have negative connotations and in applying them you effectively write off both sorts of boys.

But it is important to recognise that labels *are* often applied to pupils – 'bully', 'attention-seeker', 'class clown', and it is worth exploring what particular characteristics these labels imply.

I have listed some overleaf for 'thug' and 'wimp'.

'Thug'

shouts out
runs around the class
fights in the playground
plays in a 'gang'
works quickly and untidily
speaks or acts before he thinks

'Wimp'

quiet
never misbehaves
relates well with girls
plays on his own
works slowly and tidily
cries when hurt

When I work with managers we often look at particular individuals they manage whom they find difficult. An example that frequently comes up is the 'negative' person who can always tell you why something is unlikely to work. The trick here is to look for a positive motive for that behaviour: in this case he or she might want you to be aware of all the problems before you embark on a project, rather than stumbling upon them later. If you know the likely pitfalls then you can plan around them, so someone who spots them might be useful on the team. If the manager can view their behaviour in a different light, then he or she can respond to the 'difficult' person in a different way. Finding a positive *motive* for their behaviour provides the key to understanding how to *motivate* that person. Applying a similar thought process to the lists above, we can re-evaluate each characteristic and look for a positive quality underlying it. When we do this 'Thug' becomes 'Champ' and 'Wimp' becomes 'Charmer'.

'Thug'

shouts out
runs around the class
fights in the playground
plays in a 'gang'
works quickly and untidily
speaks/acts before he thinks

'Champ'

confident
energetic
passionate
team-player
results orientated
takes risks

'Wimp'

quiet
never misbehaves
relates well with girls
plays on his own
works slowly and tidily
cries when hurt

'Charmer'

thoughtful
respects rules
empathetic
spends time in his imagination
conscientious
sensitive

The reinterpretation of these qualities puts both sorts of boy into a completely different light: the characteristics of a 'champ' are just what many employers are seeking, and the 'charmer' will probably grow up to be a 'new man'.

NOTEBOOK

Think of the boys in a particular class. Jot down the names of any who might be 'Thugs/Champs' and any who might be 'Wimps/Charmers'.

This process of seeking positive qualities is all the more powerful if you apply it to a particular individual: only when we can view each boy's characteristics in a positive light will we be able to accept, respect and admire him for who he is. Behind many apparently negative characteristics there is a positive characteristic to be drawn out. When a teacher recognises and addresses these qualities in a boy, he will feel understood and able to live up to them.

CASE STUDY

An English teacher told me of a Year 10 boy whom other teachers found difficult in class; I'll call him Gary. Gary showed no interest in his GCSEs and spent most of his time messing around with other boys in the class. Despite this, the teacher found she liked him and wanted to see him get better grades than predicted, so she offered to give him some additional coaching in English. He took up the offer, 'I think it was the first time anyone had shown any interest in him as an individual,' the teacher explained. At the end of the year there were exams. The teacher told the whole class that she would be in school during an in-service training day, should any of them want to take part in a revision session with her. Gary was the only student who chose to give up part of his holiday to come in and revise. By valuing Gary for who he was, and letting him know that he was valued, that teacher was able to reach parts of him that other teachers had not been able to tap.

NOTEBOOK

Choose a boy you find difficult to work with. Note down his difficult characteristics on the left-hand side of a page. Reinterpret these qualities positively on the right hand side of the page.

When we do this exercise in a workshop there are always one or two examples of characteristics whose positive side it is hard for a teacher to see. It is heartening that when thrown open to the rest of the group a positive interpretation has usually been found. A boy who is rude to a teacher might be *courageous* to have spoken out; a boy who gets into fights might have a keen *sense of justice;* a boy who is devious may be *clever.* This wider, more generous interpretation does not, of course, condone unacceptable behaviour.

Any characteristic or personality can be accepted.
Certain behaviours must be limited.

When addressing rudeness, fighting or deviousness, make it clear it is the *behaviour* you find unacceptable, not the boy himself.

Example

> Instead of: 'You're nothing more than a bully. You should be ashamed of yourself! '
>
> say: *'I like you Stephen, but I'm not happy with the way you treat your schoolmates.'*

Many children who behave badly do not feel happy with themselves, and paradoxically use their bad behaviour to test out whether others like them. If you can show them that you like them for who they are rather than what they do, they will probably feel less need to behave badly. This principle can also be applied to students who seem to feel the need to prove themselves by boasting about what they can do or how much they know.

> *We talked about why he didn't like school and what the teachers said when he misbehaved. Then I asked him what his teachers said to him when he did well. He thought for a moment and then said: 'They never do.'*
>
> Debi Murdoch, Education Welfare Officer

The effect of self-esteem on behaviour

When discussing the extreme end of unpleasant behaviour, teachers usually report factors outside the classroom that cause these extremes. One group of teachers asked themselves the question, 'What is it that turns a thug into a champ, and a wimp into a charmer?' The answer, based on their experience of boys during their careers, was the boy's level of self-esteem.

$$wimp + self\text{-}esteem = charmer$$

$$thug + self\text{-}esteem = champ$$

This observation is confirmed by the Topman sponsored survey of 1344 boys.[1] Adrienne Katz and her colleagues used certain questions to indicate the respondents' level of self-esteem. They found that 25% of the sample had high self-esteem and 12% had low self-esteem, then went on to analyse the differences between these two groups, which they called 'Can-do' boys and 'Low Can-do' boys. One of the areas they looked at was attitude to school.

Some of their results are set out in the Venn diagrams below. We could re-title these charts so that the left hand one depicts our 'champs' and 'charmers' while the right-hand one depicts 'thugs' and 'wimps'.

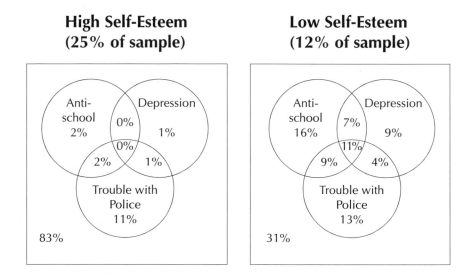

**High Self-Esteem
(25% of sample)**

**Low Self-Esteem
(12% of sample)**

4% of 'Can-do' boys were anti-school
43% of 'Low Can-do' boys were anti-school
Half the boys who were anti-school had been in trouble with the police.

2% of 'Can-do' boys suffered from depression
31% of 'Low Can-do' boys suffered from depression
18% of 'Low Can-do' boys suffered from depression and were anti-school.

69% of 'Low Can-do' boys were anti-school and/or suffered from depression and/or had been in trouble with the police
11% of 'Low Can-do' boys were in all three of these categories.

Although the researchers found that parenting style had the greatest influence on self-esteem, they concluded that the atmosphere within a school can significantly affect self-esteem by creating an ethos where boys feel valued and experience being both emotionally and physically safe: to feel valued and safe boys needed a supportive school ethos with clear rules and an effective anti-bullying policy.

Teachers have the task of moving boys into the left-hand box: firstly, by recognising the qualities of the boys they teach and, secondly, by helping boys recognise and value these and other qualities themselves. The rest of this chapter shows how to encourage a healthy sense of self-worth through day-to-day communication strategies in the classroom.

> School can significantly affect self-esteem by creating an ethos where boys feel valued and experience being both emotionally and physically safe.

How to nurture boys' self-esteem

- Get to like the boys you teach
- Set them positive expectations
- Give them a positive self-image
- Draw out their potential

Get to like the boys you teach

When my son was small, my husband had a stressful job with a long journey to and from work. On arriving home he wanted to unwind with a cup of tea and tell me about his day. Our three-year-old was having none of this: he had not seen his dad all day and wanted his attention. Each evening he became very demanding – if he could not get his father's attention himself, he would make sure his father did not get mine. My husband was not pleased at the way our son seemed to be turning out and was stern with him when he displayed this demanding behaviour.

I was in the car one day with my son when, apparently out of the blue, he said, 'Daddy doesn't like me.' I was horrified, since of course I knew his daddy loved him very much. That evening I reported the comment to my husband who was equally horrified. He went to our son and asked, 'How's my treasure boy?' The boy's face lit up and he snuggled up with his father. Their relationship changed: our son, realising he was liked and accepted, stopped his demanding behaviour; and his father, understanding his part in the dynamic, started enjoying the boy for who he was, rather than being annoyed with the way he behaved.

Boys pick up on whether they are liked and will respond accordingly. In the previous chapter we looked at how to show boys they are valued; in this chapter we have explored how to see the positive side of boys you teach. The cues boys pick up from their teachers can have a significant affect on their self-esteem: if a boy feels liked, he will believe himself likable; if he feels loved he will believe himself lovable. This sense of self in turn affects his behaviour: a boy who feels good about himself usually behaves well, a boy who feels bad about himself often behaves badly.

What the boys said

How do you know whether a teacher likes you?

They're kind and they don't tell you off much. If you do jobs for them they say 'Thank you for doing this' George, 9

You can tell. If they don't like you they shout at you more and they don't pay as much attention to you and they pick on you Ben, 10

They pick you to go up in games or read your work out (if you want to) Jack, 11

She'll probably help me out on things I don't understand Oliver, 12

They tell others off and not you James, 13

How they act, they smile, have a laugh Carl, 15

They pay attention to you more than the ones that are messing about Tim, 15

If a teacher doesn't like you, they are very picky of what you do. If I put my hand up and say the wrong answer they look to the ceiling as though to say 'You're not very bright.' I don't bother to put my hand up again David, 16

Respect is more important than like Mike, 18

NOTEBOOK

Think about the boys you teach. Are there any whom you realise you don't like? If there are, jot down their initials. Now find something likable about them and write it next to their initials. Next time you work with them, look for that likable quality and see if you can find any more. Add those to your list.

Have high positive expectations of each pupil

CASE STUDY

The new teacher could see that Marcus was very bright and she enjoyed having him in her lessons. One day she said as much in the staffroom. Her colleagues turned to her in disbelief. Was she talking about the same boy as the one they taught – a loner who showed little interest in anything in class? Well, yes she was, but the boy she taught was interested, produced good work and always contributed intelligently to class discussions. No one had told her to expect poor behaviour from Marcus, and because his intelligence was obvious to her, she treated him as an able student and he lived up to that expectation.

People have an innate desire to fulfil the expectations of those around them, and will pick up clues as to what these expectations might be. Unfortunately, we often discern subtle negative expectations from others and respond to this underlying expectation, rather than to what is actually said. For example, a small child carrying a china bowl across the room may respond to his parent's nervous warning – 'Don't drop that bowl, it's breakable!' – by dropping the bowl and breaking it. The child interprets the parent's words and tone as 'I expect you to drop that bowl' and finds himself doing so. Similarly 'Get down off that wall, you might fall!' can result in a confident, well-balanced child suddenly wobbling and falling off. The child hears his parent's expectation of disaster and fulfils it; he hears the command 'fall' and does what he has been told.

Student teachers are taught that pupils rise to the expectations of those around them and that it is good practice to have high expectations. How exactly do pupils decide what a teacher's expectation of them is? They glean it in many ways, particularly from what and how something is said to them. But what a teacher may see as setting positive expectations can all too often be interpreted as a negative expectation by pupils, for example:

As said by a teacher	As interpreted by a pupil
'Don't be late.'	'I expect you to be late.'
'If you don't improve you'll fail.'	'I expect you to fail.'
'If you carry on producing work of this standard you'll never get a decent job.'	'You're unemployable.'
'You always call out.'	'I expect you to call out.'
'Messing around again!'	'I expect you to mess around.'

Expectations negatively phrased become negative expectations, and a common response to a negative expectation is 'If that's how you see me, that's how I'll be.'

> **To be effective, expectations must be stated explicitly and positively.**

Examples

Instead of: 'Don't be late.'

say: *'I expect everyone to be sitting in their places by 2 o'clock.'*

Instead of: 'If you don't improve you'll fail.'

say: *'To get a C grade you need to carefully reread all your answers, make sure you have fully answered each question, and check your grammar, spelling and punctuation.'*

Instead of: 'If you carry on producing work of this standard you'll never get a decent job.'

say: *'When you apply for a job employers will judge you by the quality of your application. If you get into the habit of presenting things neatly it will help you get a job.'*

Instead of: 'You always call out.'

say: *'Put your hand up, then I can listen to your contribution.'*

Instead of: 'Messing around again.'

say: *'I expect you to work quietly until the bell goes.'*

Instead of: 'Stop talking.'

say: *'I would like silence.'*

Being explicit and positive leaves little room for misinterpretation by the pupil.

CASE STUDY

Wolf had been selected to represent his primary school in the City Road Safety Quiz. His mother and seven-year-old brother Arthur went along to support him. Wolf's school won the trophy and each contestant was given a goody bag at the end. When Arthur saw his brother's goody bag he became angry and tearful. Wolf and Arthur's mother had arranged to give the deputy head, Mr Leigh, a lift home. He arrived in the car park to find Arthur standing facing a wall with his arms crossed; his mother explained why he was annoyed. Mr Leigh immediately turned to Arthur and said,

'Arthur, I need someone very responsible for a very important job. I think you might be the man for the job. Do you think you may be able to help me?'

Arthur turned and looked at him.

'I need someone to take care of this trophy for me until I get home. I think you're the kind of chap I'm looking for. What do you think?'

'Yes,' said Arthur and Mr Leigh gave him the trophy to carry to the car and hold in his lap. When they dropped Mr Leigh off he thanked Arthur for taking such care and being such a help. Arthur had been holding the trophy with both hands and had not taken his hands off it from the moment it was given to him. By the time he had to give it back he was glowing with pride and he never mentioned the goody bag again.

NOTEBOOK

Rewrite the following statements as positive expectations:

a) You can take your folders home as long as you don't lose anything.

b) Don't forget to hand your projects in tomorrow.

c) Work like that won't get a Level 4 in your SATS.

d) You are always fiddling with something.

Assume these positive expectations have been met. What could you say to a boy or to the class to acknowledge this?

If you have confidence in boys' ability they will live up to it; use language that demonstrates your confidence in them.

Examples

To a boy who appears not to be trying, you might say
'I think you could do very well in this subject if you completed the work that was set each lesson.'

To a boy whose work is scruffy, you might say
'I know you like to be proud of your work, so take more time with your writing and presentation.'

To a boy who seems to be stuck on a problem, you might say
'I can see you are keen to work this out.'

To students who are arguing, you might say
'I'm sure you can work out a sensible solution to this – come and tell me when you have.'

A new little girl started at the school and she was standing next to our oldest boy at the bag hooks, looking quite scared. I said to her, 'Ben is a lovely boy and he won't hurt you. You are quite safe with him'.

He just looked at me and said, 'No one has ever said that about me before'.

Maureen Moran, *Young and Powerful* [2]

NOTEBOOK

Think of a recent situation where a boy displayed irritating behaviour in class. What could you have said to demonstrate confidence in his ability to behave well?

Give boys a positive self-image

When doing the classroom observations for this book I visited a Year 5 class. The teacher told me that I might be interested in Tom since he was horrible to other children, particularly girls, and he had no respect for female teachers with the exception of the head. I sat down next to Tom who was working at a table on his own. He asked me how to spell a word, telling me 'I'm thick, I can't spell.' I told him how to spell the word, adding, 'My Dad's very clever, but he can't spell.'

Later Tom asked for help with a question he was doing. I pointed him to the worksheet and suggested he read a particular section that would tell him the answer. 'I'm not good at reading either', he told me. We found the answer and he copied it down – incorrectly. 'My son's the same age as you,' I said, 'and I've noticed he's very observant. Are you?' Tom thought he was. 'Well the only thing you have to do to get your spellings right is look at the word and copy it exactly.' Tom rubbed out what he had written, looked carefully at the word on the worksheet and copied it correctly.

A pupil's self-image is heavily influenced by the feedback he or she receives from home and from school – family, peers and teachers. A lot of feedback is *evaluative* in that it gives the boy either a positive or negative valuation, for example: 'Good boy!' 'That's fantastic!' 'Messy work'; 'Excellent work'; 'You are rude and disruptive!' **Evaluative feedback** is usually given with the best possible intentions – to encourage a child to do better, but it has three drawbacks:

- It is unspecific about what has been done well or can be done to improve, leaving the child without guidance
- A child learns to rely on others to evaluate him and his work, rather than trusting his own assessment of himself
- Evaluative terms like 'good', 'bad', 'wonderful', 'lazy' can make a child uneasy when they do not match with his assessment of himself and so can discourage rather than encourage

Evaluative feedback can also result in negative or unrealistic responses, for example:

Evaluative feedback ➜ **possible reaction**

What a lovely picture!	No it's not, the man looks like an ape!
Clever boy!	I'll be good at everything.
You are an excellent student.	The only way from here is down!
You're so lazy.	True – so there is no point trying.

The drawbacks of evaluative feedback can be overcome by using **descriptive feedback** where the teacher factually *describes what the pupil has done* and leaves him to evaluate his work for himself.

Descriptive feedback ➔	likely reaction/self-evaluation
The figure has a real sense of movement.	I can draw well.
You got every sum right.	I'm good at maths.
This essay is well thought out and clearly presented.	I'm a good student.
You haven't completed your homework once this term.	True – I'll make more effort next time.
You left your P.E. kit in the changing room.	I'd better remember next time.

NOTEBOOK

Think of a recent occasion when you gave a boy evaluative praise. Rephrase what you said so it becomes descriptive praise.

Think of a recent occasion when you gave a boy negative evaluative feedback. Rephrase what you said so it becomes descriptive feedback.

You can encourage self-evaluation and avoid reliance on the teacher's judgment by suggesting how the child might be feeling about something instead of saying what *you* feel about it.

Instead of: 'I am proud of you.'
say: *'You must be proud of yourself!'*

Instead of: 'I am very pleased with your work, there are no spelling mistakes.'
say: *'You spelt every word correctly – I bet you're chuffed!'*

Descriptive feedback can be taken a step further to give boys a positive image of themselves by **putting a positive label on what has just been described.** Notice that this can be done even when the behaviour described is apparently negative.

Examples

- 'You drew a margin, wrote clear paragraphs and there are only two words crossed out. That's what I call **neat** work!'

- 'You did every problem yourself without asking for help. That shows **determination.**'

- 'You got on quietly with your work while I went next door. It takes **self-discipline** to do that.'

- 'I noticed you step aside when the visitor came through the door. It's **courtesy** like that which gives the school a good reputation.'

- 'The other boys listen to what you say; you clearly have **leadership** qualities.'

- 'I was disappointed to hear noise from this classroom. But on reflection I realised that it's the first time this term I've heard any noise from you. That makes you a very **reliable** class.'

NOTEBOOK

Choose a positive label to describe the behaviour below.

You've written a paragraph even though you find writing hard. That shows _____ .

You brought Jamie over to me after you hurt him in a fight. That was _____ of you.

What the boys said

How do you like to be told you have done well?

Say 'That's very well done', but describe it more, and then give me a team point　　　　　　　　　　　　　　　　　George, 9

Say 'That's excellent, I hope you can do more work like that all the time'　　　　　　　　　　　　　　　　　　　　Ben, 10

Write in my book, it's a little surprise　　　　　　　Oliver, 12

Probably to tell my parents – either in my homework book or by telling my Head of Year and the Head of Year phone my parents　　　　　　　　　　　　　　　　　　Benjamin, 13

Keep you behind to say you've done well, I prefer that to being told in front of everyone　　　　　　　　　　　　James, 13

Say so, be specific and short　　　　　　　　　　James, 16

Say it. I don't mind being praised publicly　　　　David, 16

A lot of the time, otherwise you get a bit depressed really　　　　　　　　　　　　　　　　　　　　Dominic, 18

Praise can be reinforced by telling another teacher or senior manager about boys' achievements or by writing a note to the parents or phoning them at home. Some teachers have a supply of postcards to write encouraging messages to parents. If you hear good news about a pupil you can use it to build a relationship or encourage improvements elsewhere.

Examples

- *'Miss Taylor tells me you are very funny in the school play. I'm looking forward to seeing it.'*

- *'I hear from Mr Browning that you always hand your homework in on time in Geography. Let's see if you can do the same in Maths.'*

- *'Mrs Rashid said you'd stayed behind to clear up the hall. It really made a difference having the hall ready for my after-school club. Thank you.'*

Any of these comments can be made quietly, in or out of class, or written in a note.

NOTEBOOK

Make a note of which boys might like you telling others good news about them. Who would you tell? How would you tell them? What would you say?

Another way of building a boy's self-image is to **remind him of his past successes.**

Examples

'I remember the time we were doing a project on the environment. You spent three weeks doing all the research. Then you took all the information and made it into a very imaginative display – I can still see it today!'

'Remember when you were learning your seven times table? You found it hard for weeks, but you practised and practised anyway. Then all of a sudden it clicked and you've remembered it ever since!'

NOTEBOOK

Consider a boy who is not doing well at the moment. What could you say to remind him of a past success?

Consider a class or group of boys that is difficult to work with at the moment. What could you say to remind them of a more productive time?

What the boys said

What's the best way a teacher can tell you to improve your work?

If you've done really well in one year, say 'Can you do as well as you've done last year? I know you are better than that, this isn't your best work'
Ben, 10

They've got to make you understand what you've done wrong so you can improve it
Calvyn, 14

Give the overall positive evaluative first, then say what you need to do to improve
James, 16

Say it privately, and explain how. In public I feel embarrassed and very pressured
David, 16

However much you try to see the positive side of boys, some boys come to you with a set of negative beliefs about themselves – 'I'm thick', 'I can't spell', 'I never finish my work', 'I'll never get anywhere', 'this work is too difficult for me', and so on. When boys have negative beliefs about themselves, then apparently positive or neutral comments from a teacher can result in a feeling of failure:

Boy's view of himself:	I never finish things.
Teacher's statement:	I'd like you to produce a finished piece of work this lesson.
Boy's thought:	I'm going to fail.

Boy's view of himself: I'm impatient.
Teacher's statement: It takes a lot of patience to do this.
Boy's thought: I'm going to fail.

Boy's view of himself: I'm no good at writing.
Teacher's statement: I'd like you to write a page.
Boy's thought: I'm going to fail.

What the boy sees is the gap between the teacher's (positive) expectation and his perception of his own ability; in many cases this will look and feel like a yawning chasm.

In these cases the boy needs his attention directed away from that gap, towards a small achievable step, which is then acknowledged when achieved.

Put the spotlight on what he is able to do, rather than what he feels unable to do.

Summary of positive steps:

1. Set small achievable targets

2. Describe steps in the right direction

3. Put a positive label on productive behaviour

4. Use descriptive praise to recognise larger steps

Example

Boy's view of himself: I'm no good at writing.
Instead of saying: 'I'd like you to write a page.'
say: *'Start with an idea about ...'*
then later: *'Good, you've written two lines already.'*
then later: *'You've answered the first question very clearly.'*
then later: *'Even though you're not keen on writing, you've settled
            down and written two paragraphs quite quickly.
            It takes discipline to do that.'*

Descriptive feedback is a simple and effective technique, but it does take a lot of practice to master.

The first step is to hone up your observational skills, so you are constantly looking for, and seeing, things which work.

> *Go round catching people doing things right.*
> Blanchard and Spencer, *The One Minute Manager*

The second step is to learn how to express this simply, so that pupils hear what they are doing right frequently and regularly. Once mastered, this takes very little time and has a tremendous effect on class performance and behaviour.

The third step is to recognise when you find it hard to use descriptive feedback and why. This can often be when students have 'pushed your buttons', in other words discovered what winds you up and played on it.

> *I'm good at Descriptive Praise 90% of the time, but when there is a group of boys I don't like, I find myself reverting to negative evaluative feedback. I think it's alpha-male behaviour: there's a competition on and I'm going to make sure I don't lose it. The trouble is it always ends up in some sort of confrontation.*
>
> Howard Boycott, Secondary Teacher

When your buttons have been pushed your response becomes emotional and you will not be able to look objectively for positive things, let alone describe them in a clear and concise way. Recognise your buttons, notice what happens when they get pushed, then, when they do, take a few seconds to step back and consider what to do and say. Those few seconds of silence will often make the difference between confrontation and cooperation.

> *Don't just say something, stand there.*
>
> Faber & Mazlish, *How to Talk so Kids will Listen*

> *No teacher really doesn't like you, they may not like your attitude. I know if a teacher doesn't like my attitude. Sometimes teachers take things personally, they shouldn't – the kids are only doing it to annoy them.*
>
> James, 16

NOTEBOOK

What do boys do that really winds you up?

How do you normally react when they do these things?

Given this, what would you say your 'buttons' are?

How could you react to similar situations in the future?

(It is worth women considering if there are particular male attributes that wind them up. One teacher realised that her husband is not good at acknowledging what she says at home, so when boys don't acknowledge at school this presses one of her 'buttons'.)

Draw out boys' potential

It can be very frustrating when you see pupils operating well below their ability. I once had a yoga teacher who told me I was lazy. I found myself becoming demotivated and resentful. When I asked her why she had called me lazy she explained that she thought I had great potential but she was frustrated when I didn't do each posture to the full. From then on I noticed myself putting extra effort into every pose.

If you as a teacher are frustrated with a boy's underachievement, it is easy to dwell on what he is *not* doing rather than the potential you see. The result is a self-fulfilling prophecy: a boy is told he is lazy so he switches off and produces little work. Fortunately, self-fulfilling prophecies work both ways. If you tell a boy his potential, he can live up to it. A teacher's job is to hold up a picture in front of each child of what he can achieve and then help him achieve it, step by step.

Examples

- *'Last time you wrote six lines. I think you could write eight lines this time.'*
- *You seem a responsible kind of chap to me. I'd like you to take this message to the head teacher for me.'*

Having recognised their potential, it is important that you give boys opportunities to demonstrate that potential and acknowledge any steps in that direction.

Descriptive feedback can be used to assist a student or a class to move towards desired behaviour, by describing steps in the right direction, however small.

Examples

To a boy who often runs around in class:
'All the time we've been doing this you were right next to your chair.'
or   *'You've been sitting down for five minutes.'*

To a boy whose written presentation is poor:
'These 'o's are round and the 't's are all the same height.'
or   *'Here are two paragraphs without a single mistake.'*

To a boy who works slowly:
'You were trying hard to finish by the end of the lesson.'
or   *'You work steadily at an even pace.'*

To a rowdy class that has been asked to work in silence:
'You are working quietly, now let's see if you can manage complete silence.'
or   *'You have been silent for two minutes.'*

You could also construct a ladder of small steps towards a goal in consultation with a boy or group of students, to give them an experience of success at each step.

NOTEBOOK

Identify a boy whose work or behaviour falls short of your standards, but is nonetheless making small steps in the right direction.

What could you say to him to acknowledge these steps?

Having done that, apply the same thought process to a group of boys or a whole class.

Chapter summary

How to nurture boys' self-esteem

Get to like the boys you teach

♦ Look for the positive aspects of each boy's character
♦ Tell them what you value about them
♦ Any personality can be accepted, certain behaviours need to be limited

Set positive expectations

♦ State expectations positively and explicitly
♦ Beware of implicit negative expectations
♦ Say what can or should be done rather than what hasn't been done
♦ Give them opportunities to prove your positive expectations right

Give boys a positive self-image

♦ Use descriptive feedback to encourage self-evaluation
♦ Put a positive label on what has been described
♦ Tell parents and teachers what boys have achieved
♦ Remind boys of past successes

Recognise boys' potential

♦ Tell boys the potential you see in them
♦ Describe small steps in the right direction
♦ Give them opportunities to demonstrate their potential

Chapter 4

Giving Boys an Emotional Vocabulary

All boys have feelings. They're often treated as though they don't.
They often act as though they don't.

Kindlon and Thompson, *Raising Cain*

Differences in rates of maturity between girls and boys have been well documented. Girls' verbal development is generally faster than boys', giving them a wider and more emotionally rich vocabulary. This is partly because boys spend more time in action than girls and less time communicating, giving them less opportunity to explore the vocabulary of feelings. In girls' brains, as we saw in chapter 1, the functions for emotion and for vocabulary are located in both hemispheres, with more connections between the two, while in boys' brains they are located in separate hemispheres, making it harder for boys to express their emotions.

These differences have an interesting effect on the relationship boys have with their feelings. Girls learn to recognise and name their feelings early on and so develop the ability to tell those around them how they feel. Many boys never learn this skill. Physicality, not communication, is the area they feel more at home in, and they frequently express their emotions in physical ways: playing a competitive sport, getting into a fight, hiding when feeling bad, trashing something.

Using physicality to make a point

It was the1990s, the Spice Girls were in the music charts and 'girl power' had been discovered. In the playground Alan, aged nine, found himself confronted by three girls in his class pointing their fingers at him and chanting 'Girl Power! Girl Power! Girl Power!' What could he do to stand his ground? He could think of nothing to say to stop their chanting. Suddenly it came to him, he knew exactly what would make them run. He turned round, dropped his trousers and bent over, showing the girls his two bare buttocks! They screamed and fled. Alan was so pleased by the response he had invoked that he didn't mind being sent to the head teacher's office for having 'mooned' in the playground.

As boys get older many pick up the message from the media, their peer group and their family that there are certain emotions boys are not supposed to have: what would their friends think if they were to cry, or admit to being afraid? In many cultures the only negative emotion it seems acceptable for males to express is anger. So when they are upset or afraid they feel ashamed: sometimes the shame is buried deep and the boy gives an impression of being unaffected; sometimes the shame kindles anger which is self-directed and turns inward, possibly leading to depression; at other times the anger is outwardly expressed through kicking, fighting, shouting, destroying something or being rude.

Although anger may seem an acceptable male emotion to the boy, he finds that angry behaviour is not acceptable to people around him: he is yelled at, punished and labelled as 'difficult', or worse.

Forgetting the original cause of his upset or fear, such a boy may now see adults as objects of his anger and hatred.

What the boys said

What kinds of things make you feel angry at school?

13 of the 24 boys questioned stated one of these three causes:

♦ Being told off when it's not my fault.
♦ Other people being told off when it's not their fault.
♦ The teacher not wanting to hear the full story.

If boys have done something wrong, most will see being caught as a 'fair cop', as long as they are treated respectfully. However, if they feel they have not done anything wrong, but are nonetheless blamed, the sense of injustice causes resentment that is the root of many a classroom incident. This is particularly true for students who often *do* break the rules, since they feel labelled and picked on and obliged to defend themselves when they were not to blame (or not solely to blame).

While every boy I interviewed could think of something that angered him at school, only six could identify anything that upset them. An eleven-year-old explained why:

For boys anger and upset is the same. If someone upsets them they say 'sod the upset' and get angry.

Michael, 11

Though many boys do not give the impression of being sensitive (quite the reverse in some cases) they are just as sensitive as girls and it is important to recognise this. Negative feedback can leave boys feeling stupid or embarrassed: instead of being a spur to greater efforts, it can result in withdrawal and giving up. Although boys enjoy a challenge, they may switch off if work they are set is too challenging, not wanting to ask questions in case their 'stupidity' is revealed[1].

Sometimes questions asked by a teacher, rather than throwing light on a situation, can leave a boy feeling stupid or confused, as the two examples overleaf demonstrate.

Example

In PE pupils are numbered off 'one' and 'two'. The teacher asks the 'ones' to go to the equipment on the right of the hall and the 'twos' to the equipment on the left. A boy goes in the wrong direction and the teacher asks, 'Where are you going?' He looks confused and embarrassed then runs to the other side of the hall. Had the teacher refrained from asking him a question and repeated the instruction: *'Ones to the right, twos to the left'*, the boy would have worked out which side of the hall to go to without experiencing confusion or embarrassment.

Example

In a special needs class, pupils have been asked to copy the date into their exercise books. The teacher stands between them and the board. A boy calls out, 'Sir, you're in the way.'

The teacher, looking for a more polite approach from the boy says, 'What do you need to say?' The boy looked puzzled. 'Sorry?' he ventures. 'No,' replies the teacher trying again, 'If you want me to move, what do you need to say?'

'Sorry,' comes the response a second time. *'If you'd like me to move,'* says the teacher, slightly exasperated, *'say "Excuse me, would you move so I can see the board."'*

The boy, relieved to have been told the right answer, repeats it. It would have been more effective and less painful for the boy, the teacher and the rest of the class had he simply been reminded of the necessary words in the first place.

Some teachers report becoming more aware of the sensitivities of boys as their own sons grow up: *'It was a revelation when my own* son became nine. I became aware of the range of emotions a boy of that age goes through and the struggles he had over things like homework. It completely changed the way I viewed, and dealt with, boys of that age.'

How to give boys an emotional vocabulary

- Reflect their feelings back
- Describe your own or others' feelings
- Encourage them to explore the feelings of male characters
- Give them an opportunity to care

Many boys have difficulty in expressing emotions: it is an area where they need plenty of opportunity for practice. The rest of the chapter shows practical ways to improve their emotional literacy by exploring each of the points above.

Reflect their feelings back

A child learns his first vocabulary by being given names for the objects around him; so it is with emotional vocabulary – emotions need to be given labels. Help boys recognise and express how they feel by describing the feelings they seem to be experiencing.

Examples

To some ten-year-old boys coming in from the playground:
'You look as though you have been having a really exciting time out there.'

To the 15-year-old who has not been picked for the school team:
'You practised so hard this term, you must be gutted that you are not on the team.'

Acknowledging an emotion allows pupils to accept it and move on.

Examples

To an infant class during a thunderstorm:
'It can feel scary when there is thunder and lightning.'

To a pair of fourteen-year-olds who have filled out their compass bearings worksheet wrongly due to misreading the compass:
'It's a pain to have to do it all again. I guess you'll have to put it down to experience.'

It does not matter if the boy has not come across a word before, the point is to give him a label for his emotion – as a bonus it may also extend his vocabulary.

Example

To the five-year-old boy who screws up his drawing and throws it on the floor:
'It's frustrating when a picture doesn't come out exactly as you imagined.'

Teachers often try to help pupils by offering them solutions. Acknowledging how children feel is more powerful than offering a solution because it gives them the freedom to find a solution themselves.

Example

Tyrone has no one to play with at break. The teacher observes:
'It can be lonely when your friends go and play with someone else.'
Looking glum Tyrone agrees, then he suddenly perks up. 'I think I'll ask Olly if he wants to play Star Wars,' he says and runs off to the other side of the playground.

Do not worry if you put the wrong label on the emotion, you will soon be put right.

Example

Teacher, to the twelve-year-old boy who has been stopped from beating up another:
'I can see you are really upset with Tom.'
Boy: 'I'm not upset, I'm angry! He broke my model – it took me ages to build it.'

Whilst any feeling can be accepted, certain behaviours must be limited.

Examples

– *'I can see you are really angry with Jason, but say it with words, not your fists!'*
– *'I understand that you felt I was unfair to send you out of the class, but however you felt, it is not OK to deface the walls in the corridor.'*
– *'This incident has clearly made you very angry, but you need to talk about it without swearing.'*

Boys have the whole range of emotions, but often present their emotion as anger or sullenness. These may be caused by deeper emotions such as humiliation, rejection or fear. Underlying emotions can also be acknowledged.

Examples

To a class where boys are unwilling to make a presentation:
'Most people find it scary to stand up in front of the class and speak, in fact public presentation is rated by many adults as the most frightening thing they can be asked to do.'

To a boy who has vandalised other boys' property after being dropped from their friendship group:
'You must be feeling really hurt to want to do that to them.'

NOTEBOOK

With the aim of reflecting back their feelings, what might you say to:

a) a boy who has not been picked for a special role?

b) a group of boys who have been sent to you for fighting?

c) pupils who have been given a whole class detention?

Interestingly, when I interviewed boys they had little difficulty in identifying how they felt in class.

What the boys said

Describe a good teacher:

Nice, fun, controls the class, understands you, cares for you, gives individual attention, enthusiastic, kind, doesn't shout, only tells you off when you've done something wrong, funny, doesn't favour the girls, interesting, welcoming.

How does a good teacher make you feel?

Happy, intelligent, I want to work, pleased, safe, better, ready to work, motivated, comfortable, focused, in control, reassured, I can cope.

Describe a bad teacher:

Really strict, gives you boring work, shouts a lot, tells the wrong person off, gets angry for no reason, gets cross at every little thing, stroppy, cross, horrid, they shout and screech, doesn't have any control over the class, they favour the girls, sexist, has a go for no reason, not letting you have your say, unfriendly, unhelpful, no sense of humour.

How does a bad teacher make you feel?

Bored, I can't wait till I'm out of their class, not very good, upset inside, grumpy, pissed off, scared, you don't want to work, you hate the subject, I don't want to be there, really depressed, I can't be bothered, it doesn't feel right, like I'm going to be told off, nervous, unmotivated, uncomfortable, frustrated.

Boys feel good when they are with teachers who are firm, fair and fun. When they feel good, they are motivated and tend to behave well and want to learn, when they feel bad they are unmotivated and often behave badly or don't want to learn.

Boys respond best to teachers who are

Firm, Fair & Fun[2]

A radio programme reported on a school where former army officers worked with disaffected pupils, many of whom were boys. One third of the time was spent on practical activities. The pupils were responding well. When some of the boys were asked what they liked about the scheme, this is what they said:

'They treat you like adults, not children.'
'They are dedicated.'
'You can have a laugh with them.'

Many incidents in the classroom can be avoided by adjusting your teaching style, though there will still be occasions when emotions run high. In these situations you may both need some time out to cool down before talking it through, or it may be easier for the boy to express how he feels to someone who was not involved, and this could be offered as an option.

Describe your own or others' feelings

Children learn from example and they can become emotionally literate by hearing other people describe their feelings. Teachers can play a vital role in developing boys' emotional vocabulary by stating how they feel themselves.

> *Students love personal anecdotes and boys in particular remind me years later of that dreadfully vulnerable predicament I told them I'd found myself in years ago.*
>
> John Conway, Secondary Teacher

Make sure the feelings you express are authentic and accurately described. Do you feel disappointed, sad, upset, let down, exasperated, furious, or hopping mad? The more accurately you describe your feelings the more emotionally literate those around you will become. The adjectives listed below give an idea of the range of feelings we may experience.

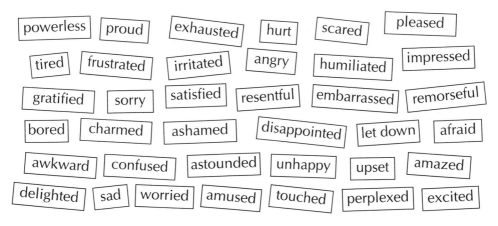

powerless · proud · exhausted · hurt · scared · pleased · tired · frustrated · irritated · angry · humiliated · impressed · gratified · sorry · satisfied · resentful · embarrassed · remorseful · bored · charmed · ashamed · disappointed · let down · afraid · awkward · confused · astounded · unhappy · upset · amazed · delighted · sad · worried · amused · touched · perplexed · excited

Such a table could be adapted for use in literacy, circle time[3], or in personal, social and health education.

NOTEBOOK

Rewrite these statements to express to your students how you *feel* about the situation:

a) This work is disgraceful!

b) You left the classroom in such a state that I've cancelled this afternoon's treat.

c) Thank you for your help.

Some teachers are concerned that they will create a bad atmosphere if they express their feelings to students; the trick is to express them and then drop them. An atmosphere can also be created by what is left *unsaid*. Most children are masters at reading adult body language and know when something is left unsaid: they may not know exactly what it is, but will make a guess and behave according to their reading of the situation. A teacher may think he is keeping his irritation to himself, but his students are aware of it in his face, his tone of voice, his lack of patience and the atmosphere in the classroom. Stating clearly how he feels gives his students a clear understanding of the situation, clears the atmosphere and allows everyone to move on. Recognising and stating how you feel whilst it is relatively minor can release the pressure, rather than bottling it up and exploding later.

Examples

- *'I'm beginning to feel irritated by all these interruptions.'*
- *'I feel terribly let down when people aren't honest with me.'*
- *'Seeing all this mess on the floor makes me really angry! I'd like it cleaned up now.'*

Make sure you *own* your feelings and don't leave the students feeling blamed for them; that would lead to resentment rather than learning.

Instead of: 'You make me feel ...'
say: *'When you do ... I feel ...'*

Teachers can also describe to students how they deal with their own feelings.

Examples

'I get so annoyed with myself when I forget something. But I've worked out a way round it: I've stuck a note on my fridge reminding me to bring in the jumble for the school fayre.'

'You know, I dread sorting out the store cupboard, it's such a mess. I've decided that instead of tackling the whole job at once I'll do one shelf at a time.'

> *'It was the fifth night running my neighbours' car alarm went off in the night. I was livid! I knew I had to say something to them, but before I rang their bell I walked up and down the street to cool off and stop myself saying something I would have regretted.'*

Students will also learn from you describing other people's feelings: *'Jack, it really irritates Ben when you sit so close to him. I don't think he likes it.'*

CASE STUDY

> *A Year 5 teacher was given a class that was known to be particularly difficult. The head warned her that they might push her patience to the limit and that, rather than blow at them, he wanted her to send anyone who misbehaved to him. She soon found he was right: not only was her patience tested to the limit, but certain members of the class provoked emotional responses in her she had not known she could have. During one such experience she said to a boy:*
>
> *'Right now I feel so angry with you for what you have done that I don't trust myself to give you a punishment that is fair. I'm going to send you to the head to decide what should be done.'*

While boys will learn from the example of all their teachers, they are most likely to look to their male teachers for role models. If boys only see women teachers express their feelings, they may conclude that this is not something that males should do.

A few male teachers have told me that they do not consider themselves particularly sensitive and are not aware of a range of emotions they feel and could express. On questioning, however, they did find they often felt angry with boys, and sometimes frustrated or let down. It is exactly these kinds of emotions that boys need to find vocabulary for to avoid aggressive behaviour at school or later in life; the 'less sensitive' male teachers would do boys a huge service by modelling responsible ways of expressing anger.

Other male teachers have explained that showing their emotions would be like making a chink in their armour that would leave them feeling vulnerable. Not that they expected the boys to take advantage of that chink, it was just that they had spent a good part of their life ensuring their armour was intact.

The interesting thing about armour is that when someone is wearing it, those around them sense that he is prepared for battle and so they ready themselves for battle too, often deciding that attack is the best form of defence. If you take your armour off you might feel more vulnerable, but others no longer feel you are a threat, so they are more able to trust you. What a gift it would be to a boy to show him he does not need armour to survive in the world.

> *If a role model gives no information about the inner world,*
> *then the youngster following that model simply fails to develop*
> *an inner world.*
>
> Steve Biddulph

CASE STUDY

A new head teacher took over a primary school with terrible behaviour problems. Within three years she and her staff had turned the school round and instilled an ethos of care and respect.

Then one afternoon a member of staff discovered money had been stolen from her handbag, the first theft in two years. The next morning the head called a school assembly and explained what had happened.

'I'm so upset and disappointed,' she told them, 'I don't know what to do.' 'We need to find out who did it,' one of the boys advised.

She considered what he had said and addressed the whole school, 'For the person who stole the money to own up will take more courage than they have ever needed in their whole life, but if they have that courage they can find me in my office.'

An hour and a half later two boys came to her office, one to admit to the theft, the other to support his friend.

Encourage boys to explore the feelings of male characters

Boys who find it difficult to admit to or express their own feelings can be asked to describe the feelings of a fictional boy or of historical or well-known male characters. Boys' stories tend to emphasise action, daring, adventure and bravado, especially when they feature themselves as the central character. It is important to allow the adventure to be told in boys' terms, but they can then be encouraged to consider how the characters might have felt at certain points in the story.

Examples

Boys can be asked how they would have felt had they been:
– an orphan in the workhouse
– a young Jew in Nazi Germany
– an evacuee
– Pontius Pilate
– Gandhi on hunger strike
– Hillary and Tenzing when they reached the peak of Mount Everest
– Oppenheimer seeing his scientific discovery used to create the atom bomb and destroy life
– Pythagoras proving his theorem
– Crocodile Dundee when he first arrived in New York
– James Bond when it looks as if he has fifteen minutes to live

Emotions can be explored and identified through discussion, role play, word-search or worksheets. Make it as fun and painless as possible.

Example

Write down three adjectives that might describe how Crocodile Dundee felt when he first arrived in New York.

Boys love heroes and value courage; history and fiction give them an opportunity to understand and value *emotional courage*: It might take emotional courage to stand up for what you think is right, to go against the crowd, to stick up for the underdog, to achieve a task against all odds, to keep going when everything looks bleak.

A soldier's life

British soldiers were drafted in to explain their role as peace-keepers in Kosovo to children exploring why people go to war over racial differences. The pupils from Saltaire primary school, near Bradford, listened intently as soldiers from the 1st Queen's Dragoon Guards described their experiences in villages affected by war and ethnic cleansing.

Speaking at a citizenship educational conference,[4] the soldiers talked bluntly about the dangers and showed photographs of wounded people, burnt-out houses and children being escorted to school. But they also talked about how they were still able to make friends among the different ethnic groups involved.

'We tell it as it is, and I hope it makes a difference to the way these children treat each other,' said Sgt Mark Waterall. 'We are not out to frighten anyone.'

Andrew Hesselwood, 11, said: 'I wanted to know more about peace-keeping. It makes me think about the way I treat others.' Daniel Parker, 11, said: 'I don't want it to happen here. I don't think it will if people talk to each other about it.'

from the *Times Educational Supplement,* 18/1/02

Studying characters such as Galileo, Nelson Mandela, Martin Luther King or the conscientious objectors gives boys a chance to recognise emotional courage. Below are some examples of emotional courage to which boys might relate.

Examples

Early in his football career David Beckham was often petulant and the opposition would purposely provoke him to bad behaviour. Over the years he has learned to use the taunts as a challenge to improve his game, whereas before they would worsen it.

As a young man the Dalai Lama refused to submit to the Chinese occupying Tibet and escaped to India by a perilous journey across the Himalayas. He set up headquarters in northern India and has spent the rest of his life promoting peace.

Oscar Schindler was a businessman who took little interest in the needs of his staff and hired Jews from the Nazis because they were cheap labour. As Schindler became aware of the horrors of Nazism, he used his business to divert Jews from the extermination camp.

NOTEBOOK

Which male characters could you use to extend emotional literacy and explore emotional courage?

Once boys understand the concept of emotional courage you can help them to apply it to their own circumstances.

Examples

- 'It takes courage to stand up for someone who is being picked on.'
- 'The more nervous you are about something, the more courage it takes to do it.'
- 'It was courageous to stick to your principles in that discussion when your mates were giving you a hard time.'

CASE STUDY

Life Education Centres[5] run a series of sessions for children from three to fifteen to educate them about the needs of their bodies and make them aware of the dangers of alcohol, tobacco and drugs. In a session with Year 5s, 'Steve' is being bullied by 'friends' to join them for a cigarette. The tutor explores with the group how Steve might be feeling. She then 'phones' Steve on a mobile phone and tells him she has some people with her who understand how he is feeling and might be able to help. She passes the phone round and the students take turns to give Steve advice on how to say 'no' to peer pressure. When the phone comes back to her she is able to add in any key points that have not been covered.

Puppet and soft toys can also be used to explore feelings. A teacher can get a glove puppet to whisper its thoughts and concerns in his or her ear and then ask the class to respond. Children of primary age think it's a great treat when the puppet joins the class and it immediately holds their attention, but older boys can also be captivated. A teacher in a unit for teenagers with behavioural difficulties had a large soft toy in circle time, which could be cuddled if a student was in need of comfort. She was surprised to find that when no one seemed in particular need of comfort the boys would argue over whose turn it was to hold it.

Example

> The Life Education Centres use a baby giraffe puppet called Harold. He is initially too shy to join the group and hides in his cupboard. Once the children have worked out what would make him feel safe (welcoming him with a smile but not too much noise) Harold agrees to come out. The children then teach Harold how to look after himself to stay healthy. When older children come back for a session they always ask for Harold, even at secondary school.

Babysitting

When my son was six our babysitter was a boy of fourteen. One evening he came round and noticed an upstairs room we were about to decorate. He recognised it as a perfect place to play football and we left the two boys having a great time kicking a ball off the bare walls. When we returned they were both asleep: our son in bed cuddling a soft toy, the babysitter on the sofa sucking his thumb. Until now we had only known the strutting, cocky, though lovable lad, the boy on the sofa was the one that his mum knew.

Give boys an opportunity to care

Have you ever seen boys when a member of staff on maternity leave brings in her new baby? The coolness disappears and macho lads soften and are heard to say 'It's so cute!' or other terms of wonder.

Boys of every age should be given opportunities to care for others: for animals, for younger people, the disabled, the old, and the infirm. There are many stories of disruptive primary age boys calming down when they are put in charge of a school pet. Schools that have a cat report a much calmer atmosphere; the cat accepts the boy for who he is.

There are excellent reports of schemes where older boys have been asked to support younger boys: in primary schools the older boys have been paired with younger boys to hear them read; in secondary schools older boys have been paired with younger boys to give them advice and support on study skills, in particular homework.[6] This not only gives the older boy an opportunity to care for another, but gives the younger one a role model of an older boy committed to learning and willing to care for others.

One primary school asked Year 6 children to support infant children during wet lunch and playtimes: the head noticed how boys who sometimes displayed anti-social and disruptive behaviour in the classroom really took to heart their infant support role.

Ways of giving boys an opportunity to care:

- school pets
- visiting the elderly
- working with the handicapped
- 'bob-a-job'
- paired reading
- peer counselling
- playing in a team
- helping in the nursery or crèche
- working on a school farm

What the boys said

Do you ever have to look after anyone or anything? How do you feel when you do?

I look after Joe at school. He's five and he lives across the road. I think he's all right if he sticks around me 'cos no one's going to do anything to him
George, 9

Next year I'm in charge of a lunch table. It makes me feel grown up
Ben, 10

I feel proud when I look after the pets because I'm being left in charge
Craig, 13

It makes you feel pretty proud of yourself
Carl, 15

I was chosen as head person on a project and I made tea for others on work experience. Both made me feel pretty important
David, 16

Some schools have set up school councils or mentoring systems where children take responsibility for easing some of the problems pupils face in school.

Examples

Sefton Education Authority has introduced the concept of 'Worry Buddies' in the Borough. Primary Schools in the scheme choose eight Year 6 children to be playground mentors. The authority provides training for the mentors in how to deal with other children's concerns and when to go to an adult for help. Staff reported a calmer playground and increased confidence in those who had received the training.

Overdale Primary School created a School Council as a forum for discussion. The school council members not only became involved as mediators in pupil conflict situations, but have helped solve strategic problems: the girls complained that the boys' football games dominated the play area leaving little room for the girls. The school council discussed the problem – until now the boys had never fully understood how the girls felt; they had just laughed when girls responded angrily. The outcome was a mutually agreed timetable in which boys had defined times to play football, leaving the yard relatively clear for more mutual play at other times.

Flour Babies

This idea has been used by schools to give students an experience of what it takes to look after a baby, and is captured in the wonderful book *Flour Babies* by Anne Fines. Each student is given a bag of flour sewn into a simple cloth casing and their task is to look after it day and night for a given number of days, keeping it intact, clean and dry. During this period they write a diary of what it is like to look after their flour baby full-time. One primary school asked their Year 6s to do it for a week, and to raise sponsorship per hour of successful caring. Their first task was to give the baby a face and 'dress' it. Parents were briefed on the project, and if asked to 'babysit' could either decline or negotiate something being done in return – the washing-up, say.

Whether 'flour babies' are on the cards or not, Anne Fines' book is a 'must read' for all teachers, giving an insight into the emotional life of boys and using caricature to demonstrate the power of teachers' communication.

NOTEBOOK

How could you set up situations to bring out the caring side in boys you teach?

Chapter summary

How to give boys an emotional vocabulary

Reflect their feelings back

♦ Give names to the emotions boys seem to be feeling
♦ Name the positive feelings as well as the negative ones
♦ Acknowledge feelings rather than trying to make a boy feel better
♦ Any feeling can be accepted, certain behaviours must be limited

Describe your own or others' feelings

♦ Tell stories of how you or others dealt with particular feelings
♦ Say how you feel yourself
♦ State how others might be feeling
♦ Describe positive feelings as well as negative
♦ Once you have expressed a negative feeling, drop it

Let them explore the feelings of male characters

♦ Study historical, fictional or famous male characters
♦ Explore how these men and boys might have dealt with their feelings
♦ Give boys an understanding of emotional courage

Give them an opportunity to care

♦ Set up opportunities to help in the community
♦ Get older boys to help younger ones with reading or homework
♦ Animals in school can bring out the caring side of boys

Putting chapters 2-4 into practice[1]

We are in a Year 10 'Small Set' English class, with eight boys and two girls. Most have learning or behavioural difficulties. Jamie has been put back a year because his behavioural difficulties resulted in him spending a lot of time out of the classroom.

The class is in an IT room and each student is in front of a PC. The task is to identify key words in certain poems, type the key words, search for an appropriate piece of clip art and insert it beneath the key word or phrase it illustrates. The task was introduced in the previous lesson and some students have completed one poem and are doing their second one. Jamie was not at the previous lesson because of behaviour problems and has not completed a single piece of work this term. The teacher wants everyone to have completed at least one poem by the end of the lesson so she can make a display.

On arrival:

> 'Good to see you back Jamie. Year 10, your attention please. This is the last session working on these poems on the computers. Next lesson we will be back in my English room where all your key words and pictures will be on display. So please make sure yours are printed out and handed in to me by the end of the lesson.'

Goes to Jamie:

> *'I see you have your key words underlined from the lesson before last. That's a good start. Type in each one then find a piece of clip art to illustrate it. Call me if you need any help.'*

The teacher goes around the class encouraging and helping others. As she passes Jamie she says:

> *'You got down to work straight away. Well done.'*

Soon she hears a disgusted 'For God's sake!' from Jamie. She draws a chair up next to him and says:

> *'Computers can be frustrating, can't they?'*

She watches him deleting everything he has done so far and says:

> *'You know Jamie; it seems to me you're a bit of a perfectionist. You are not satisfied unless everything is just right. Something I learned about computers is to save it every time I've done something small I'm satisfied with, then if something goes wrong I can always go back to what I saved.'*

She watches him typing his key words in again and asks in admiration:

> *'However did you learn to type so fast?'*
> 'I just do it', he replies.
> *'It's from practising.'*
> Jamie disagrees: 'No, I just do it.'
> *'Oh, I see, you're a natural!'*
> Jamie smiles slightly. The teacher stands up.
> *'Make sure you save it.'* She moves off.

From the other side of the room she notices him struggling to get the clip art to go into the places he wants them. He's muttering under his breath, but quietly this time.

Later she sees he has successfully put one line of pictures beneath the key words and says.

> 'You've managed to get those pictures in the order you want. It takes patience to do that. If you save that now, you'll know you have something to print out for the display. Now, what's your next key word?'

For the rest of the lesson Jamie works hard, with the odd word of encouragement from the teacher.

> 'Hey, you are really getting the hang of that.'

Five minutes before the bell he sends his page to print, then brings it to show his teacher. She says:

> 'You've completed the work before the end of the lesson. That's an interesting picture you've chosen for this key word. It will certainly look good in the display.'

At the end of the class the teacher says to the whole class:

> 'You've worked well today. Everyone has at least one thing to go on the display – talking of which I need two people to help me put the display up after school tomorrow. Would anyone like to help?'

Jamie and another student put their hands up.

> 'Jamie, Alex, thank you. If you stay after class for a moment I can write your parents a note saying you've volunteered to help after school.'

The teacher writes a note in each student's book. Jamie's note reads:

'Jamie has worked hard on the computer today and shown great patience manipulating 'Clip Art'. He has produced an interesting and colourful piece of work.

He has volunteered to help put up the display tomorrow after school. Is this OK with you? We will take no more than one hour.'

Chapter 5

Channelling Boys' Energy

'I never felt right in school. When I started school I had this sense of being trapped in the classroom; I knew I was supposed to be outside running around. That sense of wrongness never changed, even when I was in the sixth form.'

This was what a young man said when I told him I was going to write a book about boys in school. If school felt so wrong, you might wonder, why did he stay on to the sixth form? Expectations perhaps, or a recognition of the value of qualifications (interestingly he chose not to go on to university). Although few boys might be able to articulate this sense of wrongness as clearly as this young man, I believe his experience of school is common to many boys.

When exploring the difference between boys and girls in Chapter 2 we recognised that many boys are:

— energetic
— action-orientated
— physical

If the energetic nature of boys is accepted and channelled appropriately then they can thrive in a school environment. If this energy is seen as immature and disruptive, something to be suppressed and controlled, then boys will feel misunderstood, disaffected, confrontational or defiant. If they are frequently compared adversely with girls, they will feel shamed and withdraw their participation.

They don't understand why we are naughty and rebellious. They stop boys doing what boys do, so boys are forced to live a life that boys shouldn't live.   Michael, 11

Turning boys on or off education starts young, sometimes at nursery or playschool. At four or five, boys are, on average, much more active than girls, spending more time in motion and moving faster than girls, and find it harder to be still for prolonged periods.[1] Some boys are seriously disadvantaged when they start school by being asked to conform to behaviour for which they are not physically or emotionally ready. As a result their school career gets off to a bad start – instead of school being the door to new skills and knowledge it can seem like a prison, with playtimes being the only enjoyable part of the day. Negative experiences in the early years of school can set up attitudes to education and behaviour patterns for the rest of a boy's schooling and sometimes lead to behavioural or learning difficulties. The story below shows how a commonly accepted teaching method might have unintended negative consequences.

Imagine a reception class in an infant school somewhere in England. Twenty children are sitting on the carpet around their teacher. She explains that they are going to have free choice this afternoon: some will play in the home corner, some at the water table, some with the construction kit, some with the sand, some at the drawing table. The children look pleased. She tells them that she will choose the children first who can sit quietly and be still. On hearing this, most of the cross-legged children straighten their backs and look to the teacher to make sure she can see how beautifully they are sitting. One doesn't. Mitchell is in the corner next to the video player. He cannot sit still and he is poking his finger into the slot in the video machine. The teacher has already asked him to stop once and she repeats her request in an irritated tone; this is not an unfamiliar situation with Mitchell. She moves her attention back to the rest of the class.

First, she says, she will choose four children for the home corner. Who would like to play there? Six children raise their hands excitedly; Mitchell is not one of these. He has taken his fingers out of the machine, but cannot keep still and is jostling the child next to him. 'Mitchell,' the teacher says crossly, 'Leave David alone!' She goes on to select the four quietest children with their hands up to play in the home corner. 'Now who would like to play in the sand today?' Mitchell shoots his hand up and rocks forward trying to get his teacher's attention. It is the first time he has looked engaged since the children sat on the carpet. Six other children have their hands up; the teacher chooses four of them. Mitchell slumps slightly; his fingers move back to the slot in the video player. 'Mitchell, if you don't stop fiddling I won't be able to choose you.' He stops playing with the machine, but cannot stay completely still.

The process continues, the children who sit nicely are allowed to go and play; Mitchell is the last one on the mat. He is told he can go to the drawing table. He gets up slowly, and crosses the room defeatedly. The teacher notices his restraint – she normally has to admonish him for running in class – and she feels that her decision to leave him until last has already paid off.

But has her handling of Mitchell really paid off? Or has it dulled his spirit and become one of a series of incidents that will turn him off education?

In the story above Mitchell is learning that if he does not conform to the rules he will not get what he wants; the teacher also hopes Mitchell will learn that if he *does* conform to the rules he *will* get what he wants. Some boys do draw this conclusion from such an experience; others decide that they can't win, so they may as well not play the education game. Such early decisions may contribute to the high numbers of boys assessed as having special educational needs.[2]

There is no doubt that boys must learn behaviour appropriate both for school and for wider society, but we need to use methods which channel their energy without suppressing their spirit and turning them off education.

How to channel boys' energy

- Find out what turns them on
- Set them up to succeed
- Give them safe ways to express their physical energy
- Keep them stimulated and challenged

The rest of the chapter explores practical ways to apply this advice.

Find out what turns boys on

47% of anti-school boys say it's 'very true' that 'teachers don't know me as a person' compared with 26% of those for whom school is OK most of the time.

Adrienne Katz, *Leading Lads*

Who are these boys in your class? What are their interests? What excites them? Can you use this information to relate to them, motivate them or guide their study? In Mitchell's case the teacher might have used his enthusiasm for sand to encourage him, and later in the chapter I suggest another way the 'scene on the carpet' could have unfolded. The next few examples show how a boy can be motivated when a teacher understands where he is coming from.

Example

At the age of seven Conor still showed no interest in reading. His father was a storyteller who made up exciting stories for him every night. After a conversation with his teacher the mother was able to find some fairy stories from her husband's bookshelf that Conor found exciting enough to attempt to read. Both mother and teacher were amazed at Conor's ability to read complex words once he was motivated.

Example

Chris was a troubled boy, unmotivated at school, rude to teachers and frequently in trouble. A teacher discovered that he spent his holidays with his grandfather who was teaching him how to fly a light aircraft. Chris was a natural and decided he wanted to be a pilot when he grew up. His teacher explained what kind of qualifications Chris would need to fly professionally and asked if he was interested in working towards those. From that day on other teachers noticed a change in Chris' attitude in class.

Example

A geography teacher who worked in Tottenham taught the geography of Britain and Europe by getting pupils to work out how Spurs fans would get to away football matches.

How to find out what interests boys:

— Get a new class to tell you their interests

— Use English or PHSE projects to find out

— Ask individual boys what their interests are

— What do they talk about / write about / draw?

— What do they do at break time?

— Ask other teachers

— Ask boys' parents

Tim Brighouse, former chief education officer, relates the technique of a teacher he knew, when dealing with a troublemaker:

'She would bring something in for him (it is nearly always a him) related to something he privately admitted to an interest in, and saying (privately): "I saw this and thought of you." It never failed.'

Tim Brighouse, *Times Educational Supplement*[3]

NOTEBOOK

Jot down the names of boys who don't seem motivated in class.

Against each name write a list of things you know they are interested in. Devise ways of incorporating these into a piece of work. If you do not know what anyone's interests are, devise a way of finding out.

At a week's residential visit in Wales, with 24 boys and 24 girls, I offered to take a group of volunteers bird watching at 6.00 a.m. No girls volunteered. Out of the eight lads who went, three were persistent latecomers to school. All were ready and dressed when I knocked on their chalet doors at 5.45 a.m. This experience was repeated over four or five years, with similar outcomes. Boys seem to express a particular interest in natural history.

Steve Palin, Primary Headteacher

Once you know what a boy or a group of boys are interested in you can use that to devise ways of motivating them in class.

Example

A primary teacher encouraged a young dyslexic boy to write by cutting out dinosaur shapes and getting him to fill a dinosaur with writing. Once he felt more confident about writing he chose not to use the dinosaur templates any more.

Example

When the Pokémon craze was at its height a teacher noticed a boy doodling in class. The boy was drawing a monster and beneath it writing a list of qualities, in the style of a Pokémon trading card. The teacher was impressed at the ease with which the boy was filling a page with information and designed a literacy worksheet based on the trading card format.

Example

When the class studied Florence Nightingale and the effect she had on medicine, they also looked at the Crimean War and the conditions in which the soldiers would have found themselves. The boys found this more interesting, but it also provided an opportunity to explore with the class the nature of war and emotions the wounded soldiers might have been feeling.

Example

A secondary school teacher who wanted to improve the quantity and quality of homework handed in, borrowed the concept of 'study buddies' from the high school students in the TV series 'Buffy the Vampire Slayer'. In order to get the class in the right frame of mind before he introduced the idea, the teacher showed them a video of an episode of Buffy that mentioned 'study buddies'.

Author Alan Gibbons[4] uses boys' interest in football and playstation games to get them reading and exploring deeper issues. In *The Legendeer Trilogy* the hero finds himself a character in his playstation games taking part in a world of myth and legend. *Julie and Me...and Michael Owen Makes Three* is the diary – both humorous and moving – of a football-mad, love-sick teenager whose parents are separating.

Set boys up to succeed

There can be a very fine line between turning boys on and turning them off: many a special needs teacher has mastered the art of combining discipline with positive motivation and a light touch. In the reception class described earlier, rewards were being given for something Mitchell was unlikely to succeed at – to sit still for a sustained period of time. However, Mitchell could be set up to win by adjusting the yardstick for success to something more suitable for his level of development – to sit still at a requested moment. This subtle adjustment would allow him to experience a win and hence motivate him to develop his ability to sit still. The story might have unfolded thus:

In a reception class in an infants school somewhere in England twenty children are sitting on the carpet around their teacher. She explains that they are going to have free choice this afternoon: some will play in the home corner, some at the water table, some with the construction kit, some with the sand, some at the drawing table. The children look pleased.

She tells them that she will choose the children first who can sit quietly and be still. On hearing this, most of the cross-legged children straighten their backs and look to the teacher to make sure she can see how beautifully they are sitting. One doesn't. Mitchell is in the corner next to the video player. He cannot sit still and is poking his finger into the slot in the video machine. The teacher has already asked him to stop once, and explains that if he takes his hand out of the machine and he can sit still for a moment she will be able to choose him to go and play. She remembers that he loves playing with sand.

She moves her attention back to the rest of the class. First, she says, she will choose four children for the sand. Who would like to play there? Six children raise their hands excitedly, one of these is Mitchell. He is rocking and waving his hand to get his teacher's attention. 'Mitchell,' the teacher says warmly, 'If you can sit still, I can choose you to play with the sand.' Mitchell wraps his arms tightly around himself and appears to hold his breath.

'Thank you, Mitchell,' she says, 'I can see you are trying your hardest. You may go and play with the sand.' She chooses three other

children to go with him. Mitchell gets up quickly, bumping into the child next to him, and crosses the room at a trot. The teacher notices his excitement and she feels that her decision to set him up to succeed has already paid off.

It may seem unfair to give the 'least well-behaved' child his choice of activity before others who are 'well-behaved'. In fact, this is an example of equal opportunities in practice, since Mitchell is less physically mature than the other children. By being flexible, the teacher is able to set up each child in the class to succeed. She has quickly channelled Mitchell's energy into something he is interested in, does not have to spend further time addressing his behaviour, and can give the remaining children her full attention; by seeing Mitchell as a person rather than a pest, she is able to be warm and respectful. This approach is not only likely to help Mitchell, it also benefits the other children in class: they enjoy the positive atmosphere; the process of being chosen is quick and easy; they learn about respect and flexibility through example.

If it seems appropriate, the teacher might tell the remaining children that she had chosen Mitchell because he finds it hard to sit still and she was impressed to see him trying his hardest. She will, of course, also be aware of the needs of the other children in the class and devise ways of ensuring that those too are met.

Now that Mitchell has experienced a 'win' at sitting still, he can be encouraged to be still for longer periods of time as he develops this ability. This example highlights the need to be flexible in order to set boys up to succeed, and can be adapted for older boys.

Example

A teacher who found she was frequently telling boys off for talking while she was doing the register decided to change how she did it. Instead of asking for silence to take the register, she told her students they could read, draw or talk quietly while she called out their names.

Example

When the students were asked to take out or put away P.E. equipment the boys did not seem to be able to resist playing with any balls that were about. To avoid this the teacher made a point of giving balls out last and collecting them in first.

CASE STUDY

Alan knew he had been fostered because his parents did not want to care for him. A series of poor placements exacerbated his poor behaviour. Finally a loving and supportive family adopted him. His behaviour in school was frequently aggressive. His teacher spoke to the class about Alan's situation both when he was and wasn't present, and his classmates accepted his responses to classroom situations because they recognised his domestic circumstances were different from their own.

NOTEBOOK

Make a note of any rules or boundaries that inadvertently set up particular types of boys to fail.

Do your reward systems recognise enthusiasm, vigour and creativity as well as conscientiousness and obedience?

Could they be adapted to allow boys to experience success? If so, how?

THE 'COOL' READING RAP[5]

If you really want your son to read
Get him the sort of book
Some parents don't seem to see.
It's all about image and being cool
And a lot depends on what you read at school.

Bugulugs Bum Thief
Goosebumps
Point Crime
Paul Jennings
The list goes on.
At least they are not glued
To a Nintendo playing Donkey Kong.

So take my advice
And you'll feel quite proud
Please don't make them read aloud.
If you do
They'll quit reading like a flash
And your reading scheme
Will fall down with a crash.

So if you take my tips
And do everything right
Your son could be reading
By tonight!

Robert Chaseling, 11

Give boys safe ways to express their physical energy

Every teacher recognises the difference in atmosphere in school after a wet lunchtime – you can sense the undischarged energy all afternoon. It is essential to give boys ways to regularly discharge their energy, whatever the weather. Examples of this on a whole school level are:

- setting aside a boisterous play area and defining clear ground rules for the type of activities allowed in this and other areas
- allowing children outside on wet days if they have suitable clothing and their parents' permission
- letting students use the gym and hall for physical activities during break and lunchtimes
- drawing clear guidelines to distinguish between the acceptable rough and tumble on which boys thrive and unacceptable fighting or bullying
- managing the timetable so that less active lessons are followed by others demanding more activity (such as games, drama, art, technology or practical science)
- not having literacy hour immediately after an assembly, thus avoiding long periods of sitting
- if bad behaviour is a result of excess energy avoid sedentary sanctions such as staying in from play or a lunchtime detention
- timetabling a greater amount of physical activity for boisterous classes
- inviting parents or local clubs to set up lunchtime or after-school activities
- give pupils the option of sanctions that use up energy, such as litter-picking, press ups or running (even on the spot)

Individual teachers can find opportunities for boys to discharge their energy by:

— incorporating role-play and practical work in a lesson
— planning lessons with frequent changes of activity and teaching method
— giving jobs which allow movement in the classroom, e.g. handing out or collecting in books
— including physical activities in lessons, e.g. get pupils to state their opinion on a subject by going to one side of the room or another (British Members of Parliament do this on a regular basis)
— using 3-D construction in lessons, the larger the scale the better, e.g. creating a classroom-size rain forest, turning the corridor into an underwater cave

- offering a physical activity or going outside as a reward for getting work done
- giving pupils A4 whiteboards to write answers on and hold up
- when asking quick questions (e.g. in maths), throw a large soft ball to the questioned child, who returns it when the question is answered
- asking students to chant loudly (like the New Zealand rugby team). If it is not loud enough demand more volume; bring the volume down again by asking for a whisper
- using Brain Gym exercises (see box).

Brain Gym

Brain Gym exercises are simple physical activities which require concentration to get the coordination right. A well-known example is to pat your head and rub your tummy at the same time. Another is to start by writing the figure 8 in the air with your writing hand then to use your other hand to 'air write' the figure 8 backwards.

Brain gym can be used to calm a class down, either on arrival or during a lesson, to liven them up, to expend some excess energy, as a change of style, as a break between topics, as an incentive ('you have ten minutes to complete this and then we'll do Brain Gym') or just for fun.

As a bonus it is also supposed to improve concentration, coordination and increase the number of connections between the right and left brain.[6]

> *One of our strictest teachers makes us work for 45 minutes, work hard, then afterwards he'll chat to us. He's actually a hilarious guy.*
>
> James, 16

Steve Biddulph points out that when boys run around and make a lot of noise it can be an anxiety response:

There seems to be a built-in gender difference. If girls are anxious in a group setting they tend to cower and be quiet, whereas boys respond by running about, making a lot of noise. This has mistakenly been seen as 'dominating the space' in nursery schools and so on. However it is actually an anxiety response. Schools which are very good at engaging boys in interesting and concrete activities (such as Montessori schools where there is a lot of structural work with blocks, shapes, beads and so on) do not experience this gender difference in children's behaviour.

Steve Biddulph: *Raising Boys*

He also notes that schools that have started having fifteen-minute exercise sessions to start the day find that boys behave better and learn more easily.[7]

The need for physical movement was apparent when I asked boys what subjects and activities they liked best and worst. Whether boys liked a subject was more about the methods used to teach it than the subject itself.

What the boys said

Which subjects do you like best? Why? – The most popular subjects were **PE** and **Art**. The most common adjective to describe favoured subjects was **fun**.

Which are the most interesting types of lessons? – The most popular types of lesson were **practical work** and **discussion**.

'Practical' is my favourite because we move around a lot
Aaron, 12

Which subjects do you like least? Why? – No subject stood out as being particularly disliked.

The most common reasons given for not liking a subject were:
♦   Too much writing
♦   Repetitive
♦   I don't understand
♦   There's too much to take in

Which are the least interesting types of lessons? – The least popular types of lesson were writing and copying.

I don't like writing off the board, I think it is pointless
Christian, 12

I used to hate science because the teacher used to just make us copy out of books   Calvyn, 14

I hate silent work: you're left to your own devices and you don't want to ask the teacher for help in case they shout at you. Then you sit there, not doing it, and they shout at you   Tim, 15

Wrestling and Fighting[8]

On Thursday nights in the youth club I run, around 25 eight- to sixteen-year-olds gather in the village hall. By chance there are far more boys in the village than girls. Despite a clear 'no fighting' policy, very week I'd have to break up two or three 'play fights'. Then one week I tried a different tack: I laid out some mats in the corner of the hall and, pointing to them, told the fighting boys that if they wanted to fight they had to do it on the mats – anyone on the mats was fair game for a fight, anyone off the mats was not. This was the birth of the 'Bundle Corner', which was so popular and effective in channelling the boys' energy that it is set out each week. The first week it was the domain of the boys, but soon both girls and boys enjoyed it, setting up their own timetable (little ones/ middle-sized ones/ big ones, boys/girls/mixed) and rules (shoes off and certain moves not permitted). Sometimes they ask permission for a mixed age group 'bundle' and I watch the ten-year-old boys thrilled at being picked up and dropped on cushions by sixteen-year-old lads.

The application of active learning techniques with boys has been very successful. After in-service training from Geoff Hannan,[9] a teacher commented that by adapting her teaching for the boys, her Year 11 boys 'have lost their culture of failure'.

CASE STUDY

When Life Education Centres teach infants about their bodies and how to keep healthy, they use a lively interactive style where children learn through seeing, hearing and doing. Part of a session might go like this: 'We've been sitting for a long time, I think it's time for some exercise. Let's stand up and stretch. Now run on the spot. Faster! ... Stop! What happens to your heart when you run? Yes, it beats faster. Hang on, it looks like you've got balloons in your chests, have you got balloons in your chests? Well yes, you do have something in your chest that goes up and down. It's called your lungs. Have you heard that word before – lungs? Let's breathe in and say "lungs". Now shout "lungs". That took a bigger breath, didn't it? Now let's sit down and whisper "lungs".' The tutor uses the topic to excite the children and expend some of their energy, then winds them down again ready for the next piece of information.

PREFERRED REPRESENTATIONAL SYSTEMS

Neuro-lingustic programming shows that whilst people access information through all the senses available to them, most people prefer one particular representational system, either VISUAL (accessing information through seeing), AUDITORY (accessing information through hearing) or KINAESTHETIC (accessing information through feeling). About a third of a learning population falls into each category, so it is important that information is presented in away that accessible to all three types; this is often referred to as using VAK. Learning through doing is particularly important for kinaesthetic learners. Research has shown that many older 'difficult' boys can be identified as 'kinaesthetic' learners; they can be helped to succeed by using physical activities for learning. Alistair Smith's *Accelerated Learning in the Classroom* gives a broader understanding of these three representational systems.

Within a lesson an individual boy's energy can be channelled into particular tasks. Pupils who can't stop fiddling can be given a piece of blu-tac to handle, or help by sharpening pencils. A boy who finds it hard to settle can be given jobs which would normally only be given to 'responsible' pupils:

– washing the paint trays
– tidying the cupboard
– delivering messages to another member of staff
– showing visitors around the school

This has the advantage of giving the boy an experience of responsibility, but should not be used so often that he misses significant portions of his education.

I heard of a teacher who brought in a huge inflatable hammer to use in word games. When people got the wrong answer a pupil would hit them with the hammer. A lot of laughter and learning ensued.

NOTEBOOK Think of practical ways to channel boys' energy in:

♦ assemblies

♦ tutor group

♦ classwork

♦ homework

Single sex or mixed groupings?[10]

Schools have been experimenting with different groupings of boys and girls to aid learning.

A primary teacher reported how different gender groupings worked well in different subjects.

In **Science** the boys and girls were put into separate groups for practical work because of their different approaches. The boys would go straight for the equipment, pull everything out, try things out straight away and *then* work out what was happening. The girls would discuss the problem, make a plan, decide what equipment was needed and then go to get it. Both boys and girls groups worked well in their own style. But if there were mixed groups the boys dived straight for the equipment, the girls told them off for getting the wrong stuff or not thinking it through and the group quickly started to squabble.

Many boys prefer to find out things for themselves and should be given as much opportunity as possible to learn through exploration.

In **English** however the boys and girls were paired off and asked to work together, as boys' creativity and directness complemented the girls' thoughtfulness and attention to detail. Where there was written work the teacher noticed that frequently the boy thought out loud while the girl wrote down what he said.

A secondary school experimented with teaching boys and girls in separate classes for English. This was the reaction of one of the boys:

'No way is poetry girlish. My mum bought me a book of poems written by a black rapper. It's brilliant.'[11]

Robert Bruce Middle School has substantially more boys than girls in Year 8 and so decided to have two all-boy classes. They used a series of criteria to select the boys, seeing the classes as an opportunity for those boys who were underachieving as well as boys who were quiet and could get overlooked. The boys were selected to make sure each class was academically balanced. Parents were informed so that they understood the philosophy behind the single sex classes and teachers were given training on methods that suit boys' preferred learning styles. After two terms the boys are responding well to the experiment and teachers enjoy the all-boy classes, finding them particularly interesting to teach.

Notley High School, Essex has tried boy-girl 'desk partners' and found it improved the results of both the boys and the girls.
'The girls stop the boys being so easily distracted and girls chat less next to boys. In subjects like English, girls will help boys with essay planning, while in science the boys encourage the girls to be a bit more imaginative and speculative in the hypotheses they come up with.'
John Hartley, Headteacher, Notley High School[12]

Keep boys stimulated and challenged

Boy-energy is not just in boys' bodies, it is also in their minds. Their need for adventure and excitement can be met in their imagination and in the work they are given. Boys have great concentration when watching a thriller or playing a computer game; this is because the adventure is taking place in their imagination. Likewise a boy can become enthralled with a library book on sharks or karate, a project on the Roman Legions or football and the media, and with course work on Henry V or the Second World War. Select work for them that will capture their imagination and give them a classroom adventure.

Many boys baulk when faced with a blank piece of paper to fill, but find working on computers or filling in worksheets more fun and interesting. Worksheets can be made more stimulating with pictures, jokes or riddles, and an element of competition can be introduced by devising methods of self-scoring – e.g. counting the number of adjectives used.[13]

Many of the boys I interviewed said that discussions made lessons interesting. Use this to get them motivated, have a short debate about the topic you are studying, then ask students to summarise the points raised.

CASE STUDY

A newly qualified teacher was doing 'Romeo and Juliet' with a Year 10 class. The students found the language difficult and could not see the point of studying a play written four hundred years ago.

The teacher knew of someone who taught sword-play to actors and ran sessions for students on Shakespeare's plays. She invited him to run a lesson with her on Scene 1 of 'Romeo and Juliet' where the young men of the feuding families get into a fight. He arrived with two swords and spent the first part of the lesson demonstrating the finer points of sword-play. He then went through the script making sure the students understood exactly what was being said. They were astounded to discover that the boring, four-hundred-year-old script included the barracking of one young man by another about the size of his genitals.

Once they understood the script and the sword-play, students were selected to read parts and Scene 1 was enacted. The class was enthralled and Shakespeare came away with a lot of street cred.

On a radio interview a master of the choir school at King's College Cambridge was asked how they prevented choristers misbehaving. His reply was simple. 'We keep the boys stimulated and always give them challenges, then they forget to be naughty.'

NOTEBOOK

How might you approach a current teaching topic in a way that appeals to the imaginations of both the boys and the girls in the class?

What the boys said

When I asked boys what they thought of school, the word 'boring' was included in a third of their answers.

What is school like? What do you think of it? How does it make you feel?

Boring   Richard, 8

OK, people hang around in gangs in my class, but they don't really bully me. Some lessons we do are quite fun. It makes you feel older learning stuff   George, 9

Good. I'm a bit bored sometimes. Sometimes time goes fast and sometimes it goes slow   Warren, 10

The same – you go to school, work, go home; go to school, work, go home. It's OK, but sometimes the teachers are a bit unfair. That's annoying   Jordan, 10

Quite boring, but quite fun in other ways   Ben, 10

Boring   Lloyd, 10

Some subjects are fun, others are interesting, but some are boring. I think school's fun because you do lots of fun activities and make lots of friends   Paul, 11

Boring. It's quite good because you get to see your friends and you get good days like Red Nose Day and school trips   Jack, 11

Boring – you are treated as though you are stupid and get taught stuff you already know   Michael, 11

All right 'cos I've got a load of friends and I like my friends, but some of the teachers are strict   Christian, 12

OK. Some of the teachers are OK. I'm not that keen on it, but the subjects are good   Oliver, 12

Sometimes it puts you down a bit. Sometimes it's all right 'cos you look forward to your favourite lessons   Aaron, 12

Boring. It makes me feel stupid   Craig, 13

It's OK, I think. It's good to see all your friends. When you get older it gets a lot more serious in your education   Ben, 13

Boring and not fair. It's cool to be with your friends, but I don't like teachers telling you what to do   James, 13

It's mostly pleasant. There are one or two teachers that are not so nice. I'm glad to actually get an education rather than lazing around at home all the time 'cos that would get boring   Calvyn, 14

Boring, there are not enough things to do   Stephen, 14

Boring. The teachers are annoying   Carl, 15

It's OK. I don't mind going to school. I'm enjoying it more now since I chose the subjects I want to do, but there's also a lot of pressure
Tim, 15

Some things are good: the subjects I like, some teachers, my friends
James, 16

You're either committed or you're not. If you've got the right kind of teachers you can do well. I felt better as Year 11 went on because I knew I'd leave behind the subjects I don't like   Steven, 16

A nightmare. I was struggling. Every Sunday night I dreaded going. I was smiling in school, but spent every weekend down
David, 16

School is a means to an end, it's something to get out of the way. It can be a bit of a frustration or an annoyance   Mike, 18

Sixth Form is more personal. You manage your own time and you're treated more like an adult. The subjects are more enjoyable because you specialise   Dominic, 18

What can be perceived as bad behaviour is often just boys using their imaginations to make things more interesting. The teacher's challenge is to channel boys' imagination and energy into productive areas.

Example

On a school camping trip the children are erecting the tents. One of the boys notices that the fibre ribs make an excellent fishing rod, and pretends to catch a twenty-pounder. His tent-mate follows suit.

Instead of: 'Stop messing around, boys, and put up the tent!'
say: *'Looks like you're going to land a couple of whoppers there.'*
then to the whole class: *'The first group to erect their tent and pass my 'safe and tidy' inspection gets a chocolate bar to share.'*

When boys do not finding school interesting enough, they often create their own excitement by playing up. Some boys enjoy a battle with their peers or their teachers, seeing it as a challenge and a source of excitement in the day. The game is to provoke a fight and then to win it. It is important not to fall into the double trap of first allowing them to wind you up and then trying to win the battle. Stay calm and polite and look for ways of providing stimulation in the lesson.

Boys can get bored if teachers say too much; they prefer brief explanations and concise instructions and want to get on with the task quickly. They can also get bored or distracted if they spend too long at a task, and often like to be given short time-frames.

Examples

> *'I'd like you to write three paragraphs. You have ten minutes to complete them.'*

> *'Write down five things you remember from the last lesson.'*

> *'If there was a quick and easy way of doing this would you like to know what it was?'*

Some boys find a lot of instructions or a large task overwhelming. Many respond better if given a single task or instruction, then another one once that is completed. This principle can be used to motivate boys to do project work, asking them to produce one part of the project at a time.

When boys' interest is aroused they can be extremely imaginative and creative. Boys like a challenge and enjoy competition. Their interest can be aroused by using language like:

- *'Bet you can't...'*
- *'No one I know has managed to do this before.'*
- *'Find ten uses for...'*

Computer or **sporting** language can be used to encourage normal classroom activities: *'click'* on to a word; *'save'* to listen; *'print'* to write (all the better if commands can be given in robot-like voice); a sentence written can be a *cricket run,* a paragraph a *boundary,* and a whole page a *six.* Children can try to hit the teacher for six by writing a page! Using contemporary boys' language can help to engage them.

Example

A teacher wrote this note in a boy's exercise book:
'You seem to have slackened off work while I was away. Now I'm back I would like to see a lot more effort put into your homework. Deal?'
Underneath the boy had written, 'Deal!'

A dull or 'uncool' task can be reframed as exciting or challenging to get a boy's cooperation.

Example

At the lunchtime table-tennis club a teacher spots a sweet on the floor at one end of the table. It looks as though it will be squashed at any minute by the player at that end. The teacher motions to a boy who is waiting to play.
'I've got a dangerous job for you,' she whispers. The boy's ears perk up.
'Do you see that sweet at this end of the table?' she continues, pointing to it. *'Could you swoop in and pick it up without getting run over?'*
The next time the table-tennis ball goes wide the boy runs and picks up the sweet, then returns beaming to the teacher.
'I knew you could do it!' she exclaims, *'Would you put it in the bin over there.'* He does.

If boys are to thrive in schools then their energy must be at least accepted and channelled; how wonderful it would be if it were also welcomed and celebrated!

NOTEBOOK

You want boys to complete a page of work. How could you make this sound exciting?

Think of a boy who needs a challenge. What task could you set that would be achievable but stretching? How could you make it sound exciting?

Chapter summary

Channelling boys' energy

Find out what turns them on

♦ Find out the interests of everyone in the class
♦ Ask pupils, parents and other teachers
♦ Notice what they talk about, write about, joke about
♦ Relate the topic being taught to boys' interests

Set them up to succeed

♦ Choose ground rules which take account of boys' energy
♦ Be aware of the development and abilities of each member of the class and treat them accordingly
♦ Reward enthusiasm and vigour as well as conscientiousness and obedience

Give boys safe ways to express their physical energy

♦ Get boys outside as often as possible
♦ Include a variety of activities and teaching methods in each lesson
♦ Use role-play, discussion and 'practical' in lessons
♦ Devise learning experiences which include physical activity
♦ Use physical activity as a reward for getting work done

Keep boys stimulated and challenged

♦ Recognise the imaginary worlds boys often inhabit
♦ Select work which will capture their imagination
♦ Set stretching but achievable challenges
♦ Use concise instructions and short time-frames
♦ Describe ordinary tasks in exciting ways

Chapter 6

Boundaries and Discipline

Good discipline contains a boy and his energy, providing a sense of physical and emotional security he needs in order to learn the larger lessons of self-control and moral behaviour.

Kindlon and Thompson, *Raising Cain*

A boundary is the line between acceptable and unacceptable behaviour. Boys need clear, firm boundaries; the harder they push against them the stronger those boundaries should be. It is important to remember, however, that part of the purpose of boundaries is to give them something to push against, so don't be surprised (or angry) when they do just that! As a head teacher said to parents at a secondary school open day:

'We have a strict uniform policy. One of the reasons we do that is to give the students something to rebel against.'

How to maintain boundaries

- Ensure students know what they are
- Apply them fairly and consistently
- Use positive language to reinforce them
- Acknowledge when students stay within them

This chapter explores how to put these four points into practice, then goes on to look at the nature of effective discipline for boys.

Ensure students know what the boundaries are

Students feel safe when they know the limits of acceptable behaviour and what sanctions apply should those limits be broken. School rules and disciplinary procedures serve this purpose: particular departments (e.g. PE or Languages) may have ground rules specific to their subject; particular events may require special ground rules (e.g. a school trip); individual teachers may have particular rules in their class. In order to make sure students are clear about where they stand, rules and sanctions should be clearly defined, communicated and agreed. The agreement can be done verbally, or by asking pupils to read and sign the rules. It may work to involve pupils in making rules: in some junior schools each class discusses and agrees on class rules at the beginning of the year; some secondary schools use the School Council or Year Councils to agree on rules.

Displaying rules prominently ensures they are absorbed even if they are not consciously read. This even applies to non-readers: if rules are written up and pointed out clearly to young children, possibly with a picture for each rule, they will be able to tell you what each rule says, even though they cannot read every word. Another important benefit of writing the rules up is that they become independent of the teacher: when a teacher refers to a rule or applies a sanction the pupil is less likely to take it personally, nor will the teacher take it personally if pupils point out that the teacher has broken a rule!

Wherever possible rules should be stated positively and simply, for example:

'We expect members of the school to care for one another'

'Registration is at 8.45 a.m.'

Occasionally rules may be phrased in the negative; if this is necessary keep it simple, for example

'No spitting'
'No hitting'

Some Liverpool schools even manage to phrase these positively with the rule:

'Keep your hands, feet and insults to yourself'

> For me 'rules' all come down to the same thing – respect. When I meet a class I tend to only introduce the expectation of respect for each other and then gradually introduce other rules as they arise, showing how they all relate to respect. I don't find it productive to swamp them with lots of seemingly disconnected rules at once.
>
> John Conway, Secondary teacher

Apply boundaries fairly and consistently

For students to respect boundaries they must see them being applied fairly and consistently. Boys are particularly sensitive to the perceived injustice of teachers apparently favouring girls. The cry of 'it's not fair' can do more to undermine a rule than almost anything else. If one of the class rules is 'no interrupting', for example, then anyone who interrupts should be reminded of the rule. Do not fall into the trap of allowing a few interruptions at the beginning of a discussion to get it started, then reprimanding those who interrupt once the discussion is in full flow. Beware also of allowing Janet to interrupt because she is usually well-behaved and makes useful contributions, but rebuking Kevin for interrupting because he always does.

Boys and girls tend to push boundaries in different ways. Often a girl will subtly step outside a boundary and, because she has a less confrontational approach, her behaviour draws little attention. A boy, on the other hand, tends to be more 'in your face'; it is often because of boys' behaviour that the boundary is drawn in the first place, and when they overstep the boundary they usually draw attention to themselves. Nonetheless, once a boundary has been set, it is important that it is seen to apply to both girls and the boys.

What the boys said

Do teachers treat boys and girls differently?

Fifteen of the 24 boys I interviewed felt that girls were treated better than boys at school. This is what some of them said:

Normally the teachers say 'the girls are acting better than the boys today'   Richard, 8

Whenever we move into a new year the teachers always think the boys are bad and the girls are good, so they're automatically mean to the boys and nice to the girls   Jordan, 10

Teachers give girls more respect. Male teachers are more even, but female teachers are sexist   Michael, 11

I'd prefer it if the teachers treated the boys better by not shouting when they say they've done something wrong   Christian, 12

To a girl they say 'Calm down', to a boy they bellow 'Why don't you be quiet!'   Oliver, 12

One teacher gives a warning if girls are talking, but if boys are talking he doesn't   James, 13

They always ask boys questions and never the girls
                                                      Stephen, 14

CASE STUDY

A teacher had set up a series of lunchtime Circus Skills Work-shops in the school hall. The response to the first workshop had been good, and a lot of students had come to learn. During the second session, the interest dropped off: the same number of students came, but while one group practised to improve their skill, another group were chatting and messing about. The teacher made a ground rule that if students wanted to come to a session they had to spend the time practising circus skills.

On the third session fewer students came and the atmosphere was more productive. The teacher noticed two boys sitting on the stage chatting. He went up to them and reminded them of the ground rule that any students attending the workshop had to spend the time practising circus skills.

'So what is it to be, boys,' he asked with a smile, 'in the hall practising circus skills, or going outside?'

He didn't get an immediate response to his question. One boy grinned and said 'Oh, Sir!' while the other looked surly and muttered, 'It's not fair, we were only talking!'

The teacher noticed a girl sitting watching the others practising. 'Lucy,' he called, 'the rule is, if you are in the hall you practise circus skills. Do you want to join in here or go outside?' Lucy thought for a moment: 'I'll go outside, Sir,' and got up to leave. The teacher returned to the two boys.

'So what is it to be, boys,' he repeated, 'in the hall practising circus skills, or going outside?' Both boys looked slightly

surprised at Lucy's departure, and the teacher, knowing one of them had a soft spot for Lucy, expected them to follow. To his surprise, both opted to stay. They immediately joined in the activity and after ten minutes practice were calling the teacher over to admire their new skills.

NOTEBOOK

Make a note of any rules that girls get away with breaking but boys don't.

What could you do to avoid that?

There will be occasions when fairness and consistency have to be overridden by doing what works best in particular circumstances. Of course teachers must use their own judgment in such cases. The important thing is to make a conscious choice and understand your reasons for doing so.

Example

A teacher was having an informal and light-hearted conversation with his students. He made a teasing remark to one of the girls who, before she could stop herself, responded as though to one of her friends with 'Oh, piss off Sir!' As soon as she realised she had said it, she looked horrified, slammed her hand over her mouth, then apologised. The teacher asked her to see him after the class and carried on with the lesson. After the lesson he told her that such language would normally result in a detention. In this case he felt that the informal nature of the conversation had led to her swearing by mistake, and on this occasion he had decided not to give her a detention. But, he reminded her, he did not want to hear that language in school again.

In this example the teacher had decided to make an exception to the rule, not because the offender was a girl, but because the circumstances seemed exceptional; and the fact that she had to stay after class to hear the 'verdict' meant that other students did not feel she had got away with it.

We should be told off, but they shouldn't go on about it and over-explain. After they have told you off they should drop it, some teachers remain moody afterwards.

David, 16

Part of fairness is being seen not to hold a grudge. Some pupils feel that when they are told off the teacher does not like them and that can affect their relationship in the future. Teachers can prevent this by pausing after a rebuke, then smiling or making a positive comment to signify that the offence has been dealt with and no grudge remains.

Examples

After giving a rebuke or a sanction, a teacher might say, in a firm and friendly tone:
– *'That's that dealt with, let's get back to the business in hand.'*
– *'O.K. telling off over. Where were we?'*
– *'If we put the matter we have just discussed to one side, I'm pleased with the improvement that I have noticed in your work recently.'*

CASE STUDY

A Year 10 boy was misbehaving in class and the teacher asked him to move seats. She had a sense that he was pretty frustrated and that it would have been better to ask him to stand outside and have a chat with him. But she was frustrated too and didn't have time for that. He got up reluctantly, and as he did the table rose and hit another pupil.

At this point the teacher lost her temper and told him that if he could not behave then she would rather he didn't stay in the lesson. The boy was angry and humiliated and as he left the room he told the teacher to 'fuck off'.

As a result of this he was suspended for three days. Aware that she could have handled the situation better herself, her next concern was how to bring him back on board and help him participate willingly on his return.

The first time she saw him in the corridor she made a point of smiling and raising her eyebrows as though to say 'I've forgiven you, can you forgive me?' She repeated this each time their paths crossed. When he came to his next class with her he grinned.

'We both caught each other on a bad day last time we met,' she said. 'Yeah, and I got suspended for three days,' he replied, and grinned again.

They both knew that the hatchet had been buried.

Why boys are excluded

'It is not usually the worst pupils who are excluded. Exclusions continue to be a mystery to me.'
'Exclusions appear random.'

These quotes appeared in an MBA on managing boys' achievement.[1] A passage in Steve Biddulph's book *Manhood* may throw some light on them:

One wise woman teacher put it like this:
'Every boy who has been expelled while I was at this school did so in the following way. They got into a fight with a man teacher, who sent him to another man teacher, who irritated the boy more. It became a matter of will with no room to back down.'

In this teacher's opinion exclusion had been less related to the original offence than the way it had been dealt with.

Use positive language to reinforce boundaries

Once boundaries are known, applied fairly and consistently, and seen as independent of the teacher, then they can be used in a very positive way. Then the pupil does not have to take it personally when his teacher reminds him of a rule, and the teacher need not take it personally if a pupil breaks a rule. A pupil can be reminded of the rule calmly, through the use of clear, positive and impersonal language.

Example

Instead of: 'I'm sick to death of having to tell you to put your blazer on!'

say: *'The school policy is that blazers should be worn'.*

Example

The rule is 'no interrupting'. When Paul interrupts Amber, the teacher can:
- *say nothing and point to the 'No interrupting' rule*
- *turn to Paul with her finger to her lips and say 'As you were saying, Amber'*
- *state clearly, 'We have a "No Interrupting" rule in this class'*
- *say 'We'd be glad to hear your point of view, Paul, when Amber has told us hers'.*

As long as the teacher maintains a non-judgmental tone of voice throughout Paul will get the message: 'I am accepted and respected, but I must stick to the rules.'

What the boys said

If a teacher has to tell you off, what's the best way for them to do it?

Not shouting at me all the time. Just saying, 'Warren, you shouldn't do that   Warren, 10

Tell me off by myself not shout across the room because it's quite embarrassing   Paul, 11

Send you outside and come out and speak to you with the door open so the teacher can hear the class, but the class can't hear the teacher   James, 13

Boys recognise that they need to be told off from time to time, but they do not like being shouted at, and notice that teachers seem to shout at boys rather than girls for apparently the same offence.

Acknowledge when students stay within boundaries

When boys break rules they are likely to receive the admiration they desire, either from other boys or from girls who enjoy their display of daring. Therefore it is important that boys also experience a pay-off from sticking to the rules; teachers can provide this with praise and acknowledgement when they notice boys staying within the boundaries that have been set.

It is essential that the acknowledgement is sincere so it cannot be interpreted as sarcasm, also that it is low-key to avoid embarrassment.

Examples

In the 'No Interrupting' example above, when Paul puts his hand up the teacher might say,
'Thank you for waiting your turn, Paul.'

At the end of a discussion a teacher might comment,
'Thank you all for respecting others' comments. We could all hear and enjoy them.'

There is a 'no jackets in class' rule, which particular boys often have to be reminded of. At the beginning of a class, the teacher notices that all jackets have been taken off, so remarks,
'It's good to see that everyone has taken their jackets off.'

Actions and consequences

When boundaries are broken, then sanctions usually apply. The purpose of sanctions is not to punish, as is so often imagined, but to teach self-discipline and encourage social behaviour in future; and sanctions should be designed with this in mind. Boys respond best to a non-confrontational approach to discipline and to being rebuked privately. Public reprimand leaves them smarting with humiliation and often evokes a 'couldn't care less' response. More importantly, it leaves them with the desire for revenge – they dream of reversing the humiliation, inflicting it with interest on the teacher: forty years after the event, my husband still expresses his animosity towards a teacher who humiliated him at primary school.

Discipline should be:

- **respectful**
- **fair**
- **appropriate**
- **consistent**

Used well, discipline will build character and conscience; used badly, it creates enemies and teaches brutality. It is worth putting a little thought into selecting sanctions that are consequences rather than punishments.

Example

A group of boys find a muddy patch in the playground and have a mud fight.

Instead of: giving them an extra homework of writing down ten reasons why throwing mud is dangerous

get them to: *clear up the mess they have made in the playground*

Example

The school fayre is next week. There is a banner on the school fence advertising it. Two boys fighting by the fence tear the banner.

Instead of: giving them a detention

get them to: *arrange with the DT Department for them to mend the banner themselves*

It may take more thought and supervision to apply 'consequences' rather than punishments, but as boys become more aware of the consequences of their behaviour, they will become more responsible about what they choose to do and less time will have to be spent on discipline in the long run.

NOTEBOOK

Think of an incident where a boy reacted to being given a sanction by becoming rude and uncooperative. Review what was said and done before he was rude. Put yourself in his shoes: Was there anything that might have seemed unfair or disrespectful to him?

What might have been done differently to avoid this reaction?

Afterthought – the use of questions

In disciplinary situations questions are often used to get to the bottom of a misdemeanour. Questions should be used carefully, however, since some actually do more harm than good. During my years as a trainer I have observed that the mind seems to respond in one way when it is given information and in another way when it is asked a question.

When people are given information the mind goes into 'receive' mode; when they are asked a question the mind goes into 'response alert' mode. On issues of discipline it is usually more useful to have boys' minds in 'receive' rather 'response alert', since the latter is likely to result in defensiveness. Avoid, in particular, questions like:

– *'Who did that?'*
– *'What are you doing?'*
– *'Why did you do that?'*
– *'What did you do that for?'*

These questions provoke a defensive response in people of any age. 'Who did that?' provokes an automatic response, in many, of 'It wasn't me!' whether it was or it wasn't. 'What are you doing?' often provokes the answer 'Nothing'. 'Why did you do it?' or 'What did you do that for?' provoke a wider range of unhelpful responses, spoken or unspoken, such as 'Because I did', 'To get a laugh', 'Because I hate school', 'Because I'm bad', 'Because I'm a loser', 'I can't answer this question, I feel stupid'.

On issues of discipline it is best to replace such questions with statements or expectations.

Examples

Instead of: 'Who did this?'
say: *'I'd like this cleared up by the end of the lesson.'*

Instead of: 'Why did you do it?'
say: *'Thank you for being brave enough to admit to doing this. You know that it is against the school rule x, and the sanction for this is y.'*

This approach is clean, clear and respectful. It combines a fair discipline with an acknowledgement of the boy's qualities; it is likely to leave the boy feeling good about himself, good about his relationship with the teacher and less likely to break the rule in future.

What's the matter?

Elliot had had a fairly troubled term, but things seemed calmer recently. Then one day he completely lost it. Instead of rebuking him the teacher asked, 'What's the matter, Elliot?' Elliott burst into tears and explained to the teacher that he had found out from the hospital that he had to have a major operation.

Boys often behave badly when they feel bad inside. The question 'What's the matter?' acknowledges this, implies that the behaviour was atypical, and allows the boy to recognise why he is behaving in that way.

Chapter summary

How to maintain boundaries

Ensure pupils know what the boundaries are

♦ Display rules prominently
♦ Don't have too many
♦ Keep them simple

Apply rules fairly and consistently

♦ Ensure pupils see rules being applied to girls as well as boys
♦ Make it clear you do not hold a grudge

Use positive language to reinforce boundaries

♦ Speak calmly, avoid shouting
♦ Instead of dwelling on the misdemeanour or asking questions, remind pupils of the boundary:
   – 'the rule is...'
   – 'the school allows'

Acknowledge when pupils stay within boundaries

♦ Give boys a pay-off for sticking to the rules
♦ Praise the whole group publicly
♦ Praise individuals privately

Sanctions should be

♦ seen to be fair
♦ appropriate to the misdemeanour
♦ applied respectfully

Chapter 7

Humour and playfulness

On the mantelpiece...a word had been written on the dust! ...The word was a transitive verb, an exclamation, a command, of which an exact English translation is impossible. The closest equivalent probably would be the phrase: Lighten up!

Tom Robbins, *Jitterbug Perfume*

Boys are often mischievous, they like the rude and the ridiculous, they like to have fun. Schools are an ideal place to have fun as long as the humour can be channelled constructively. But, like their energy, boys' humour is often seen as inappropriate, immature and disruptive – something to be suppressed rather than channelled.

Take the example of a ten-year-old boy in a drama lesson. The teacher has asked the class to do an exercise to loosen up their facial muscles; this involves contorting their faces into different shapes. One of the boys starts sniggering. The teacher notices and asks, *'What's so funny, William?'* 'Your face looks like an alien, Miss,' he replies candidly. This is too much for the teacher, she reprimands the boy for his insolence and tells him to stand outside the class.

This raises an interesting question: was the boy merely seeing the humour in the situation or was he being rude? We will never know: sometimes boys joke simply because they see the funny side, sometimes they purposefully use humour as a 'wind up' or to hurt or offend, and often they are prepared to risk offending for the sake of a good joke. They take this risk because they believe the object of the joke will brush it off in the same way the boy himself might brush off a fall if he tripped in the playground.

She went ballistic – it was hilarious!   Michael, 11

It is useful for teachers to remind themselves that they will often get unexpected responses in class, and to prepare themselves to deal with these benignly. Responding to boys' humour in a way which neither demeans them nor escalates the situation takes a degree of generosity: the teacher must be prepared to assume the boy's intentions are good – as they often are.

The following 'four rules' can help teachers respond to boys' humour:

— *Assume a playful intent*

— *Don't take things personally*

— *Respond playfully (where appropriate)*

— *Acknowledge humour, encourage all to laugh, then move on*

Sometimes boys' humour is *meant* to wind you up. If you don't allow it to then they will soon stop trying it on.

The 'alien' incident would have been avoidable if the teacher had been able to see the humour of the situation she had set up and not needed to ask what was funny. She might simply have said: *'Our faces do look funny, William, but try to do this without laughing.'*

If she had asked what was funny and been told she looked like an alien she would have been wise to see the humour of the boy's observation without taking his comment personally and simply acknowledged the humour of the situation. Even if his response had been meant as a wind-up, her calm response would show that the wind-up had failed. If she had decided to respond playfully she might have used this sort of approach:

'I look like an alien and you look like a... let's think now... (to whole class, lightheartedly) *What does William look like?* (responses and laughter). *Now everyone look at the person next to them and see what they look like while continuing your own exercises.'*

Or she may have brought an element of playfulness into the exercises by asking pupils to turn to a partner, *'smile your widest smile, then make your longest most serious face – try not to laugh!'*

Humour is sometimes seen as disruptive, something which distracts from a lesson. The atmosphere created by humour, however, can make a lesson more enjoyable and hence increase the amount of learning that takes place.

If a teacher tries to suppress students' laughter, it often results in distracted whispering and giggling and little learning. It is most productive if the humour can be shared with everyone and used to enhance the atmosphere. Once the humour has been released, move on.

Example

| *'You have ten seconds to laugh at this... Time's up!'*

It is worth having some techniques up your sleeve for dispelling hysteria. The techniques used for getting silence in a group often work, especially those that require the pupils to copy a series of movements, since this moves their mind on to something else. A familiar but not too easy 'brain-gym' exercise might do it. If a class finds it difficult to calm down after a joke then, rather than avoiding humorous situations, spend a few minutes agreeing on a 'calming down routine' for the next time.

Burping and farting

What's invisible and smells of bananas? *A monkey's burp!*

Whenever we discussed boys' humour on courses the issue of 'body noises' arose. Burping and farting provoke hilarity amongst boys at almost every age. Farting can be most disruptive since the response to it is prolonged by the smell taking its time to permeate the room, often causing lively recriminations from one side of the classroom to the other.

Teachers agree that if ignored it often results in uncontrollable giggling, and many found that a humorous response was most effective. One teacher would say 'It wasn't me!', another would open the window dramatically, saying 'I think we need some fresh air in here!'

A secondary teacher's strategy was to look concerned and earnestly ask whether the boy needed to go to the toilet. The laughter stopped immediately. (This approach could work if asked either seriously or playfully, but would not work if the tone of voice conveyed any ridicule or disrespect.)

In a primary class a boy's fart caused his friends to laugh uproariously at him. He was so embarrassed and angry that he stormed out of the room. Whilst he was out it would have been a perfect opportunity to discuss embarrassment with the class and explore the different ways people deal with it.

> What goes 'Ha ha, bump? *A boy who's laughing his head off.*

Students and teachers report that often the funniest teachers also have the firmest discipline; the pupils are aware of the firm boundaries within which sometimes quite riotous humour takes place.

CASE STUDY

Mrs. Jackson was in the hall doing PE with her class. It was the end of the lesson. Suddenly she heard shouting outside the window. She looked to the window and saw Mr. Noble, who was due in the hall next lesson, surrounded by his class. He was leading them in a chant, 'Let us in! Let us in!'

That man's crazy, she mused to herself, but they do love him. She asked her class to stand in line and went to the door to let the other class in. There was going to be bedlam in a minute. They tumbled in smiling and laughing. Mr. Noble raised his arm to the ceiling and yelled, 'Freeze!'

There was silence, each one of his class frozen in whatever posture they had been in when he spoke. 'Thank you Mrs. Jackson, thank you class,' he said, 'Now line up in silence over there,' pointing to the side of the hall Mrs. Jackson's class wasn't. They did, without a murmur.

Sometimes humour is inappropriate to the occasion, but even in such a case, in order to move on, it is often more effective to acknowledge the humour rather than attempt to suppress it.

Example

Instead of: 'That's not funny!'

say: *'I can see you two are having a good joke, but now's not the time.'*

Making an investment

The language was getting so bad in class that the teacher had instituted a swear box – ten pence a swear word. A boy came up to the teacher and asked how much he owed. 'Sixty pence,' was the reply. 'Right,' said the boy, pausing to make a quick calculation, 'fuck, cunt, bugger, shit. Here's a pound, Sir.'

Boys often use humour to 'take the mickey' out of one another. Sometimes this is just fun, other times it is a subtle form of bullying; sometimes it is genuinely meant as fun but is very hurtful for the 'victim'. Teachers have a great opportunity to educate children about humour – style, content, impact, appropriateness and timing. A twenty-minute 'lesson' on humour might make the class easier to teach for the rest of the year.

NOTEBOOK

Make a note of any boy whose humour winds you up. Explore the humour from his point of view.

Think of a time you could have responded more playfully to boys' humour. What might you have said or done?

Use your boys' liking of humour to motivate them in other areas:

– Put comics and joke books in the library or reading corner
– Make a display area where jokes can be pinned up
– Have a joke box with a weekly prize for the best joke (rather than reading them all yourself get pupils from that class or an older class to judge)

- Get pupils to put a riddle up for a week and give a prize for the right answer
- Offer a five-minute joke session at the end of the lesson as a reward for hard work

> Why is a garden like a story?   *Because they both have plots.*

Using humour effectively

Research shows that people think more creatively when they are enjoying themselves. Whilst planning this book I discussed some of the ideas with a man in his early twenties. When I suggested that teachers should use humour as a teaching tool, he responded that in all his years at school he had never come across a teacher with a sense of humour. I was surprised and saddened by this, since in most staffrooms there is laughter and joking and many teachers have a fine sense of humour. Nonetheless, given this young man's experience, it is worth asking whether this wealth of humour is taken into the classroom.

> *A funny teacher grabs your attention. It's a more relaxed atmosphere and there's rapport.*   Mike, 18

A teacher is a performer and audiences respond well to humour. When teachers do take their humour into the classroom, it is important that it is the type of humour students should be emulating. Staff rooms are noted for a degree of healthy cynicism and the humour that goes with it. In one school I visited, motivational posters had been displayed around the school; it was in the staffroom, not the corridors, that the posters had been defaced with witty annotations. Whilst such humour may be needed to keep staff sane, it is unlikely to be a great example for students. Boys appreciate classroom humour and will copy the style used, so it is worth considering what effect you want your humour to have, both first hand on the class, and second hand when boys borrow your style to use on others.

How to use humour effectively

- Be an example of constructive humour
- Humour should not be at anyone's expense
- Use humour appropriate to the age of your audience
- Take care with sarcasm

Be an example of constructive humour

Humour and playfulness in the classroom lightens the atmosphere, makes learning easier and teaching more fun. Every teacher will use humour differently, depending on their personality, the situation and the students involved.

> I have five apples in one hand and six apples in the other, what do I have? – *Big hands!*
>
> James, 13

What the boys said

Do you have any teachers who make you laugh? What do they do?

She goes to the cupboard and pretends to cry and says 'I'm going to tell my mummy!' George, 9

They tell jokes Paul, 11

He jokes around with us. He's sarcastic with us, but if we're sarcastic back he gets angry Christian, 12

They act. Our history teacher talks about death and murder and we go 'Ugh!' He told us these people had their heads cut off by a guillotine and could still speak afterwards! Oliver, 12

They make the odd comment to make the subject more cheerful for you Ben, 13

He made fun at everything, but it wasn't nasty. One day we were guessing his age. It was my birthday and when I guessed too old he said 'It's your last birthday!' Calvyn, 14

There aren't many teachers that make me laugh; it's good if they do, but not many have that talent Tim, 15

Spontaneous humour, like if a teacher draws something and someone says it looks like something else. Teachers who can take the mick out of themselves. They should only take the mick out of a pupil if they know they can take it James, 16

The teachers respond when the pupils have a laugh Steven, 16

CASE STUDY

Two of the boys I interviewed were raving about a particular English teacher. 'She makes everything fun and funny,' they said. I arranged to observe her teach. These are some of the things she did:

She had a strong, firm voice and body language, smiled a lot and often had twinkling eyes. She had a warm smiling face when listening.

When a boy was talking whilst she took the register she said, 'Ben, I expect silence.'

When she found people hadn't done their homework, she asked the class, When was your homework to be handed in?' They replied, 'Tomorrow'. 'Today!' she announced dramatically, with a smile. On one table she found that no one had done their homework. 'What!' she exclaimed in mock horror. The students understood their omission was serious, even though the communication had not been heavy.

When a boy seemed not to be listening, she said 'Nick, what have I just said?' and gave him a big grin. To a boy who was slouching she whispered, 'Craig, sit up'. When the class responded enthusiastically to a question she said 'Please don't all speak at once, I can't hear.'

Having explained to the class that she wanted each person to do a one minute presentation, she said, 'I'm going to be very, very kind to you – I'm going to give you a few minutes to prepare!' Before the first presentation was made she said to the class,

> *'Can you give this person who stands up your full attention!'*
>
> *At the end of the lesson everyone was standing behind their chairs and making a lot of noise. She said, 'Year 8, that was really lovely, the way you were standing before. Can I see that again please!' There was immediate silence.*

There are many ways to lighten the atmosphere in the classroom. One way is to tell funny stories; some other ways are described below.

Example

The teacher at fire drill puts on a sergeant major voice:
'Right class, we have a fire drill. Line up by the door in double-quick time. Down the stairs to the playground, Liam lead the way. Qu-ick march!'
The class do what they are told with grins on their faces – quickly, silently and safely.

Example

A teacher working with a Year 1 special needs group explains that she is about to give them some instructions and asks, *'Have you got your listening ears on?'*
She and the children point to their heads and in unison say *'Thinking caps off!'* and pointing to their ears say, *'Listening ears on!'*

Example

A teacher explaining the homework standards he expects, adds:
'The last boy who gave in untidy homework was found in a shallow grave behind the playing fields!'
The students gasp in mock horror. The point has been made in a memorable way.

Example

To a child who doesn't leave big enough gaps between his words:
'Those poor words are all squished together, they haven't got room to breathe!'

Example

To playfully express her disapproval, a teacher says:
'The next person who does that will be hung, drawn and quartered!'

Example

To a seven-year-old boy who has done a set of maths questions very quickly:
'You tore through those questions like a rocket going to the moon.'

Example

When a pupil responded to a teacher with a grunt, she would mimic the grunt in two different tones, saying:
'Now, was that an "uuh" or an **"uuh"***?'*

Example

A history teacher is explaining that facts can be misinterpreted. To demonstrate this he asks, *'What is a floor?'*
'The floor is something you stand on,' someone replies. The teacher leaps up onto a table, and pointing towards his feet, says, *'Floor.'*
'No it's not!' choruses the class. He goes on to ask, *'What is a chair?'* 'Something you sit on,' he is told. He drops to the floor, points to where he's sitting, and says, *'Chair.'*
The class will never forget that lesson.

Example

The art cupboard is frequently left in a mess, the teacher sticks a note to the door.

> *I feel so despondent*
> *When I'm left in a mess*
> *If I ask you for tidiness*
> *I hope you'll say 'Yes!'*
>
> *The Art Cupboard*

Example

For homework a class were asked to pretend to be a Roman Consul and write an election speech that would persuade the citizens of Rome to vote for them. Once written, they had to make the speech look as though it had been found on an archaeological dig. Suggestions from the teacher included running it over, dragging a wet teabag over it, scrumpling it up, burying it in the garden and setting fire to the edges. The homework was much enjoyed and the speeches were pretty good too.

Example

Some teachers have a puppet as a companion. The puppet 'whispers' in the teacher's ear and the teacher tells the class what it said. It can be brought out at any point to lighten the atmosphere or encourage good behaviour. *'Charlie wants to come out, but he's waiting for you to sit down.'*

You can give the puppet a personality. It may be very cheeky and say or do outrageous things that the teacher pretends to disapprove of: *'Char-lie! I can't tell them that, it's rude! You want me to tell them? Oh, alright then. Charlie said he's not playing till you're all on your bums!* Or it can be used to explore issues: *'You don't want to do maths today, Charlie, because you don't think you're any good at it.'* The class can give him advice on how to get better at maths.

In a review[1] of Sue Cowley's *Getting the Buggers to Behave* Chief Education Officer Tim Brighouse remembers a teacher who had several glove puppets, each with its own personality. If the class had a bad reputation, she would take Sooty, a puppet with attitude. When Sooty suddenly appeared from behind the teacher's back to shout 'Bollocks!' at Year 9, the outraged teacher would ask: 'What did you say?' Sooty would even do some marking, but his language was not allowed to stray to quite the same extent on paper.

Example

One secondary school teacher gave the board rubber an identity – Eric the Eraser. The teacher would tell his students stories of what Eric had got up to on in-school and out-of-school adventures. Teenage boys loved having the extra personality in the classroom.

Example

Some teachers are good at caricature and accents and act out different characters to the class. One infant teacher used a different hat for each character. He would go out of the door and then come back with a particular hat, accent and character. When the character left the room the teacher would come back in and the class would yell, 'Sam's been in here doing spellings while you were out!'

Games lessons?

I had a crazy maths teacher in Years 7 and 8. Each row was a team and won or lost stars. Then in 'Pink Elephant Week' we all had to put our hands on our heads each time he said 'Pink Elephant'.

Each lesson was based on some kind of cartoon. He used to take the mick out of silly questions in the maths book. He had a Homework League: you got two points if you didn't do your homework, then the next time you got one extra point and a card with a one hour maths problem on it.

James, 16

Humour and playfulness can be a powerful tool to change the atmosphere, and may be used to defuse a situation before it gets unnecessarily heavy. Imagine what would happen if a teacher, instead of delivering a lecture when half the class hasn't done the homework, falls into the character of one of the aliens in the TV programme 'My Parents are Aliens', and talks to his or herself in wonder about the strange priorities on Planet Earth – how earthlings prefer to stand in front of a piece of shiny material coating the head with gungey stuff (gelling their hair), rather than find out how spacecraft work so they can travel to other galaxies. The class will certainly be listening, will remember what you said, and may even be amused and impressed enough to do their homework.

Change a mood, not a mind.
> Faber & Mazlish, *How to Talk so Kids will Listen*

Example

The angry boy yelled at the teacher: 'You're an old tart!'
'I very much object,' she said pointedly, *'to the word ... old!'*
The boy burst into tears. At Christmas his teacher gave him a box of tarts.

Humour should not be at anyone's expense

Kieran was an energetic seven-year-old who loved to fight; he wanted to be able to kick-box, so asked his parents if he could learn a martial art; they enrolled him in a local karate class. Karate suited Kieran well since it channelled his aggressive energy in a very disciplined way; the teachers were strict but kind, and he flourished under this regime. By the time he was ten years old he was near the top of the class and the teachers treated him as a senior student, someone who should know what's what.

Then one day he came home from a class and announced to his parents he wanted to give up karate – the teachers, he said, made fun of him when he made mistakes and he did not like being made a fool of in front of other people. His parents explained that because he was one of the higher grades, his teachers were using humour to tease him like they might an older person – they meant no harm. Kieran was not persuaded; he never went back.

Humour at another's expense is unproductive and potentially damaging. The laughter it engenders is mixed with discomfort and a sense of relief that someone else is the butt of the joke – this time. Constructive humour, on the other hand, is inclusive; it encourages everyone to laugh together and lightens the atmosphere.

Boys often 'jokingly' tease one another and they need to be shown that getting laughs should not be at someone else's expense.

Humour about oneself can be very effective, as long as it does not demean you. It's good to be able to make a joke when you make a mistake, or laugh when what you draw or something you say comes out wrong.

Boys respond well to anecdotes about a funny predicament you were in, and respect the fact you are able to laugh at yourself. They will also learn from the example.

Try pressing the Rewind button

Faber and Mazlish[2] suggest that when things go wrong we give everyone a second chance by 'rewinding' and replaying the scene in a different way. You can introduce it by first using it yourself: *'That's not what I meant to say, I think I'd better rewind. Right, what I meant to say was...'* Later give students the opportunity to rewind: *'It sounds like you might want to rewind, Steve. Let's go back to the beginning. '*

Once students understand the concept it can be used to defuse quite explosive situations: Jerry comes in late and you confront him for it; he loses it and swears at you. You respond by saying, *'Jerry, neither of us did that very well. I think we need to rewind. Why don't you come in again and we'll see if we can do it better next time.'*

Instead of the videotape 'rewind' you can also use the film makers' 'cut' and 'take two'.

Use humour appropriate to the age of your audience

In the earlier example, the karate instructors were using humour with a ten-year-old that teenagers and adults might have appreciated (though they, too, might not have enjoyed being made fun of). What is considered funny by five-year-old boys may not be by nine-year-olds; what makes a boy of eleven laugh could be viewed as pathetic by boys of fifteen; and the subtle irony of staffroom humour is likely to be lost on all but the sixth form. Since boys are younger than their teachers, their humour will be, by definition, less mature. They and their humour will mature in time, but while they are a particular age or maturity, rather than judging their humour, why not drop down to their level and enjoy it?

> *I often start lessons with a young kid's joke: 'How do you kill a circus? –* Go for the juggler!' *Kids groan, but it sets a light tone and gets attention.*
>
> Mike Shankland, Liverpool Hope University

When I spoke to teachers about what made boys of different ages laugh, this is what we came up with:

WHAT MAKES BOYS LAUGH   * universal

5 years   slapstick*, visual/physical, funny noises*

7 years   rude things, toilet humour*, zany humour

9 years   jokes and joke books ('knock knock', 'doctor doctor', what did the x say to the y?', 'what do you get if you cross x with y?')

11 years   destruction, practical jokes, simple word-play, swear words, rudeness, gory things, funny stories*

13 years   genitals*/physical attributes, personal comments about adults/teachers

15 years   sexual innuendo, irony, banter

What the boys said

What makes you and your friends laugh?

We tell jokes to each other and people do silly things George, 9

Rude things Warren, 10

When you are playing games and something stupid happens Jordan, 10

When you are naughty it makes you laugh Ben, 10

Funny stories, when my friends tell jokes or funny stories or do something stupid Paul, 11

Jokes, funny stuff that Dad says, when he uses swear words funnily Michael, 11

We like messing around, we laugh at everything Christian, 12

Things they do and say Oliver, 12

Jokes Craig, 13

Stupidity is really funny, when people are mucking around Ben, 13

Jokes about women, and fights Carl, 14

Sarcastic humour is the funniest when it's light-hearted Tim, 15

Anything Stephen, 16

Being around your mates, banter and situational jokes David, 16

Universal things, like things going wrong. When teachers say wrong things or have peculiar phrases Dominic, 18

Not everything that boys find funny is appropriate for the classroom and one of the tasks teachers have is widening a boy's repertoire. Valuable discussions could be had with a class about the effects of different kinds of humour and the importance of timing – a skill that would stand many people in good stead later in life.

Take care with sarcasm

Consider the following definitions found in the Reader's Digest *Oxford Complete Wordfinder:*

Sarcasm 1 A bitter or wounding remark.
2 A taunt, especially one ironically worded...
Synonyms: irony, scorn, derision, ridicule, venom;...

Irony 1 An expression of meaning, often humorous or sarcastic, by the use of language of a different or opposite tendency.

Sarcasm is sometimes used as a tool to maintain control in a class, particularly with teenage boys. Since teachers are intelligent and articulate, a well-constructed piece of sarcasm can put a boy firmly in his place and hence appear a very effective tool. The danger with it, however, is that the recipient is left waiting for an opportunity to get his own back – and, rest assured, he will.

By its very nature sarcasm can be ambiguous and wounding. Consider the boy who is always last, to whom a teacher says 'It's nice to see someone with such a good relationship to time.' If the boy takes the words at face value he will consider the comment a compliment and miss the point; if he understands their real intent he will be left confused and hurt. Neither effect is helpful or constructive, nor is it a good example for the students.

Banter and irony, on the other hand, can be great ways of bringing fun into the classroom, particularly with teenagers who are masters of these forms of humour (and of sarcasm). There is a very fine line between banter and sarcasm, and the way to test it is to check whether the humour is belittling anyone. The delivery is crucial: a remark made with a smile and a twinkle in the eye will be interpreted benignly; a change in the tone of voice can change banter to a cutting remark.

Teachers can have a great influence on the way boys use humour, since they will inevitably copy what they hear from their teachers. Be an example of playful, constructive humour and this will rub off on your pupils.

NOTEBOOK

Think of an irritating situation that occurs in your classroom on a regular basis.

How could you respond to that situation in a humorous way in keeping with your personality?

What the boys said

Are your teachers ever sarcastic? What's that like?

12 out of 24 boys said 'Yes', seven liked it and five did not. This is what they said:

It's not mean, it's funny   Richard, 8

They say 'You've been good today' and I say 'Yes' and then they say 'No you haven't'. It's confusing and quite annoying Ben, 10

I like it because I'm always sarcastic and it makes me feel like the teachers are a bit like me   Christian, 12

Some of them have a sense of humour where they can be sarcastic. It's a change from being completely stern   Ben, 13

Our best teacher is sarcastic, but then she says 'Only joking!'
                                                            James, 13

There's one who's sarcastic in a funny way. That's enjoyable, you know the teacher's having a laugh   Tim, 15

It's OK if it's a joke. If I'm not in the mood I don't really like it and think 'I don't need that right now'   James, 16

If a teacher made a sarcastic comment then I switched off. One said 'You are not doing very well. If you work like this you won't get anywhere in life'   David, 16

I had a history teacher who was sarky and patronising. He'd show you up in front of the class, so I was less likely to input to the lesson   Mike, 18

It's quite interesting; it can be amusing   Dominic, 18

Chapter summary

Responding to boys' humour

♦ Assume a playful intent
♦ Don't take things personally
♦ Respond playfully (where appropriate)
♦ Acknowledge humour, encourage all to laugh, then move on

How to use humour effectively

♦ Be an example of constructive humour
♦ Humour should not be at anyone's expense
♦ Use humour appropriate to the age of your audience
♦ Take care with sarcasm

Chapter 8

Ten Ways to Avoid Shouting and Nagging

Frequent criticism and rare praise create a negative atmosphere. So do excessive use of loud reprimands, sarcasm and aggressive reactions to minor offences. And if the male teachers are the ones who shout, it is the women, we were told, who are seen to 'nag, nag, nag'.

Kevan Bleach, *Raising Boys' Achievements in Schools*

When all else fails parents and teachers alike resort to shouting or nagging. Their aim is to obtain co-operation, but a common result is to create disaffected youngsters. The natural response to being shouted at or nagged is to 'turn the volume down' – switch off, phase out, watch the movement of the lips and wait for it all to be over. Students listen just enough to understand what the noise is about and extricate themselves from trouble, but the rest is just a dull background murmur – it is too painful, humiliating and embarrassing to tune in properly.

I made a point of shouting very rarely, I'd save it. Then on the few occasions I did shout it was usually about safety and the children really took notice.

Shirl Klein, infant teacher

What the boys said

How do you react when teachers shout?

I think 'Oh no, she's going to tell me off'. I feel like I want to swear in her face   George, 9

Whatever she shouts at me about I won't do it   Jordan, 10

I just look at them. I say 'Yes, yes, yes' unless I haven't done it. Then I argue   Ben, 10

In my head I'm thinking 'Shut up'   Christian, 12

I think 'Whoa, calm down'   Oliver, 12

I answer back. I get annoyed if I haven't done anything wrong   Craig, 13

When teachers have control they don't usually need to shout   Ben, 13

'What me? It was him!'   Stephen, 14

I shout back   Carl, 15

If I don't like the subject I can get reluctant to work   Tim, 15

It's OK if I deserve it. If I don't then I respect them less and think 'How can you be so petty?'   James, 16

If it's serious you say 'OK, sorry', if it's not you have to have a go and say 'It wasn't me'   Steven, 16

I feel humiliated, embarrassed and resentful, so I switch off   Mike, 18

Part of the job of parents and teachers is to train the next generation, whether it is to be respectful of their environment, to care for each other, to keep their agreements or to be conscientious in their work. In the training process one thing is sure, that children won't do what you have asked them every time and that they will need frequent reminding. However, reminding can often turn into nagging if one is not careful. You can avoid shouting and nagging by:

– limiting what you say
– keeping it positive

This chapter sets out ten strategies for gaining boys' co-operation without nagging or shouting. Many of the ideas in this chapter are based on the work of child psychologist H. Ginott, and authors and parenting experts Adele Faber and Elaine Mazlish; they can be extremely effective after a little practice.

1. Set clear rules

Boys like to know where they stand. If rules are clear and fairly applied then any incursions can be dealt with swiftly. To use rules effectively:

– set clear rules
– apply those rules fairly and consistently
– make sure you are an example of the rules you set

The first two points are covered in Chapter 5. The last point is also important, since students learn as much, if not more, from the *behaviour* of their teachers as they do from what their teachers *tell* them to do: when a teacher yells at a class 'Keep the noise down!' the pupils may be learning that it works to shout; a teacher who demands that students respect each other must take care to show respect for every student.

When Paul was 6 years old he was with his father when they were caught speeding. His father handed his licence to the policeman with a £10 note in it. 'It's OK son', his father said as they drove off 'everyone does it.'

When Paul was 8 he sat in on a family meeting discussing how to reduce their income tax. 'It's OK kid, everybody does it,' said his uncle.

When he was 9 his mum took him to the theatre but there were no seats until his mother gave the attendant a fiver. 'It's OK son, everybody does it,' she said.

When he was 12 he broke his glasses on the way to school. His aunt convinced the insurance company they had been stolen and got £50 back. 'It's OK,' she said, 'everybody does it'.

When he was 15 he made the school rugby team, and the coach showed him how to hurt the other players without the referee seeing. 'It's OK,' he said, 'everybody does it'.

When he was 16 he worked at the market and was shown how to put over-ripe tomatoes beneath the ripe ones in the shoppers' bags. 'It's OK,' said the stallholder, 'everyone does it'.

At college he was not a great student, so when he was offered the exam questions for £10 because everybody does it, he took them. He was caught, and sent home in disgrace. 'How could you do this to us?' said his dad, 'you never learned anything like that from home!'

Anon.

2. Use a gesture

One very effective way of communicating is to use gestures instead of words. It makes pupils listen with their eyes.

Examples

If a rule is being broken *point to that rule* on the notice.
If someone is speaking out of turn *put your finger to your lips.*
If someone is speaking too quietly you can *put a hand to your ear.*
If someone is sitting on the desk you can *point to the chair.*

A series of gestures can be agreed in class with particular meanings that everyone in the class understands.

Examples

– Four figures pointing to the floor means put the legs of the chair on the floor.
– A teacher who knew deaf and dumb sign language taught his class some of the signs.
– A teacher working in a special unit for teenagers with behavioural difficulties used to hold her nose when she thought she smelled 'bullshit'. Her students responded well to being caught out in this way.

3. Say it in a word

In *How to Talk so Men Will Listen* Marion Woodall points out that for women the purpose of communication is often to build a relationship, hence the habit of using a lot a detail to create context and intimacy. For men, however, the purpose of communication is more often to exchange information; men prefer facts and are irritated by what seems unnecessary detail. This also applies to

boys: keep what you say to them short and to the point – an effective way to do this is to just use one or two words.

Examples

To a boy with a jacket on in class: *'Jacket'*
To a boy breaking a rule: *'Rule 3'*
To a boy who forgets to close the door: *'The door'*
To a boy sitting on a desk: *'Your seat'*
To a boy who forgot to use margins: *'Margins'*
To a boy who has dropped litter: *'Bin'*

To be effective these should be said firmly and calmly. Notice that the main word chosen is a noun, not a verb, and it is being used more as a reminder than as a command. Using verbs in the imperative is likely to be seen as controlling and so provoke a negative reaction, for example 'Sit!' 'Move!' or 'Stand!' The command 'freeze' is used very effectively in drama classes, but its use would have been explained at the start of the course. People often ask whether these one-word reminders should be followed by 'please'. As long as a respectful tone is being used, the word 'please' is not needed. Tone of voice is often more important than content: a harsh or abrupt delivery of a command such as 'Quiet please!' can completely negate the respect implied by the word 'please'. When a student asks a question, a single word may also be the most effective answer.

Example

The class are playing rounders. A student is caught out and asks the teacher, 'Do I stand out or should I be fielding?'
Instead of: 'I spent ten minutes at the beginning of the lesson explaining the rules. Weren't you listening?'
say: *'Fielding.'*

4. Give information

Boys learn at a very young age to protect themselves from perceived attack. Being told off by a figure of authority is almost always perceived as an attack and boys often react either by shutting down or aggressively defending themselves. To avoid these reactions teachers can replace a rebuke with information that will enable boys to cooperate.

Examples

Instead of:	'Why have these books been left in such a muddle? You really are a messy class!'
say:	*'Text books go in a pile by the door, exercise books are to be left on my desk.'*

Instead of: 'Who made this mess on the table?'
say: *'Dirty paint palettes are washed in the sink.'*

Instead of: 'You are all staying in for ten minutes after class.'
say: *'We will go as soon as the room is tidy.'*

5. Describe the problem

Simply describing a problem can allow boys to work out for themselves what behaviour is required.

Examples

Instead of: 'Late again!'
say: *'This is the third time this week you have been late for my lesson.'*

Instead of: 'Why haven't you done your homework?'
say: *'The homework is due in today.'*

Often, describing what you see or hear is sufficient.

Examples

Instead of: 'I asked for silence!'
say: *'I can still hear talking.'*

Instead of: 'I can't believe the state of this classroom!'
say: *'There is paper all over the floor.'*

Instead of: 'Stop shouting out.'
say: *'I don't see any hands up.'*

6. State how you feel (and then drop it)

If teachers feel angry or frustrated they often express it by shouting or nagging. An excellent way to avoid this scenario is to express how you feel explicitly.

Examples

Instead of: 'You left the classroom in such a state yesterday that I've cancelled the treat we were going to have this afternoon.'

say: *'When I came in and saw the state of the classroom yesterday I was disappointed and upset.'*

Instead of: 'This work is disgraceful!'

say: *'I get really frustrated when I see a student of your ability produce such untidy work.'*

Students are often surprised to find out the extent to which teachers care, and will change their behaviour as a result. Once you have stated how you feel, it is important to draw a line under it and move on.

7. State positive expectations

When expectations are not being met it is useful to restate them.

Examples

Instead of: 'This is disgraceful work!'

say: *'I expect a much higher standard of work from you.'*

Instead of: 'Here we go again, there's always someone who comes unprepared!'

say:	*'I expect everyone to come to my classes with a pen, pencil, ruler and rubber.*
Instead of:	'What do I have to do to get you to hand your homework in on time?'
say:	*'I expect all my students to hand their homework in on time.'*

Looking at all the circumstances when introducing certain expectations for the whole class reduces the need to nag or shout at particular individuals. For instance, some boys find it difficult to listen if a speaker does not grab their attention, such as a pupil who speaks quietly. Many teachers set an expectation that students should listen respectfully to one another; but this is more likely to be fulfilled if you also set an expectation of reading loudly. If children were expected and encouraged to read loudly it would help their confidence, at the same time making it easier for others to pay attention.

8. Point out what needs to be done

When things are not right it is tempting to dwell on the negative, but this is a major turn-off. It is more productive to focus on positive action – what can be done to put things right and what benefit will there be? This gives boys a guideline and an incentive for action.

Examples

Instead of:	'Who made this mess?'
say:	*'Let's get this mess cleared up.'*

Instead of: 'You won't leave the classroom until this mess is cleared up.'
say: *'As soon as this mess is cleared up you can leave.'*

Instead of: 'Of course you fell off if you rode with no hands!'
say: *'To stay on your bike keep your hands on the handlebars.'*

Instead of: 'You'll fail if you don't work.'
say: *'You're more likely to pass if you do your homework.'*

9. Put it in writing

The written word can be a very effective form of communication because it does not have a level of volume or tone of voice. Notes can be written on the board, pinned up in the classroom, written in an exercise book, handed to a boy or duplicated and given to each member of a class. The teacher has time to think about what needs to be communicated and pupils have time to consider it for themselves.

Examples

Before a class outing a message goes up on the board:
Meet in the car park tomorrow at 9.00 a.m. Bring a packed lunch and a jacket.

A note by the art room sink might say:
Wash dirty palettes and stack them on the shelf.

A teacher prepares a set of 'praise slips' to be put on students' desks as they work: *'Neat Work', 'Good Concentration', '100% Correct'* etc. This allows for quiet praise and is something the student can keep, or not, as he wishes.

A lunch-time five-a-side game in the gym got out of hand. Later a teacher handed out two stapled sheets of paper to everyone who had been playing. It said: *Students are welcome to play 5-a-side in the gym at lunchtime as long as there is an independent referee with a whistle. A whistle can be borrowed from the school office. A copy of the rules of 5-a-side is attached.*

In a noisy classroom, a teacher one day simply went to the board and wrote the words: *Silence is golden.* There was immediate quiet. This may not have worked a second time!

10. Brainstorm the problem

If there is a recurring or intractable problem then it is worth taking some time out with the pupils involved to explore the problem and look for possible solutions. The time invested in sorting out the problem is reaped many-fold by its absence in the future.

Here are some guidelines for brainstorming:

— Choose a time when any emotions have subsided
— Allow sufficient time for the exercise
— Write down the problem as precisely and impersonally as possible
— Ask for possible solutions to the problem
— Tell participants the three rules of brainstorming:
　1. Think of as many imaginative solutions as possible.
　2. Any idea put forward is written down.
　3. No comments must be made on ideas until all have been written down.
— The teacher can add ideas too

- Once all the ideas have been written down, each idea is assessed as 'Workable', 'Possible', 'Unworkable'
- The group then uses the 'workable' and 'possible' ideas to come up with a practical plan to solve the problem

Example

Despite a 'hands up' rule many of the boys in a class shout out and interrupt. The teacher's various attempts at getting the boys to put their hands up before making a contribution have failed, so he decides to have a brainstorming session. He writes up the problem on the board and explains the process to the class. This is what was written up on the board at the end of the brainstorming session:

How to get everyone to put their hands up before speaking:

- Change the rule
- Interrupters get sent out of the class
- Pelt interrupters with rotten tomatoes
- Boys should be more self-disciplined
- Girls should speak louder
- Sir turns his back on the class when he hears shouting
- Clap when we haven't got our hands up
- Put rude sticker on the forehead of shouter-outers
- Everyone chants 'hands up' at interrupters
- Give shouter-outers a yellow card
- If you get three yellow cards in a lesson you get detention

Each idea was then assessed, and the following plan agreed:

- *If someone speaks without putting his or her hand up, the class chants 'Hands up!' twice.*
- *If that person does it again, he or she receives a yellow card.*
- *Anyone with three yellow cards in one lesson gets a detention.*

In the event the 'Hands up!' chant was usually enough, and although yellow cards were given out occasionally, no one received three in one lesson.

What if this doesn't work?

If you don't get cooperation through one approach, simply try another. For example, if you want students to put their hands up rather than call out:

Set clear rules: *make it a class rule*

Put it in writing: *put a 'Hands Up!' sign at the front of the room*

Use a gesture: *finger to lips/hand in the air/point to the sign*

Say it in a word/phrase: *'Hands up!'*

Give information: *'I'll take answers from students with their hands up.'*

Describe the problem: *'I hear a lot of answers but I don't see any hands up.'*

State how you feel: *'I feel bombarded when you all yell out at once.'*

State expectations: *'I expect hands up from those who have an answer.'*

NOTEBOOK

In what situations do you find yourself most likely to:
– nag boys at school?

– shout at boys at school?

What might you do or say to avoid nagging or shouting in those circumstances?

Chapter summary

10 ways to avoid shouting or nagging

1. **Set clear rules** *Rule: Litter goes in the bin.*

2. **Use a gesture** *Point to the bin.*

3. **Say it in a word** *'Bin.'*

4. **Give information** *'Litter goes in the bin.'*

5. **Describe the problem** *'There are sweet papers on the floor.'*

6. **State how you feel** *'I find it very frustrating to have to remind you to put litter in the bin.'*

7. **State positive expectations** *'I expect everyone to put their litter in the bin.'*

8. **Point out what needs to be done** *'All that paper needs to go in the bin.'*

9. **Put it in writing** *A note on wall reads 'Litter in the bin please'.*

10. **Brainstorm the problem** *Define the problem: litter is not being put in the bin. Write up as many imaginative ideas as possible. Agree on a workable solution.*

Chapter 9

Parents as Allies

We lay great stress on keeping in close touch with parents, so that from school we may gain insight into the child's home. Only in this way can we come to understand each child... for instance, we may notice a trait in one child that looks the same as a trait in another; yet the meaning of that trait may be altogether different in the one case than in the other.

Rudolf Steiner, *The Kingdom of Childhood*

The way a boy behaves at school can be greatly influenced by his parents and it is important that teachers and parents work together to bring out the best in boys. Unfortunately there are many obstacles to a good working relationship between parents and teachers.

Conversations between a parent and teacher should, one might think, be a straight-forward, rational meeting of two adult minds with the common purpose of reviewing a boy's progress or finding strategies to improve his behaviour in school. In fact such conversations can be emotional minefields.

Parents' perceptions

Many parents feel uncomfortable in school. It brings back their own experiences as children, reminding them of difficulties with teachers which they had in the past. They may remember feeling stupid, resentful, trapped or angry. Even where the school experience was good, the hierarchical relationship with teachers they once had may still colour their present parent-teacher relationship, leaving them feeling at a disadvantage with a teacher.

Parents often feel that any deficiencies in their child are seen as their fault, so that a teacher's criticism of their child is by implication a criticism of their parenting ability. For some parents this would result in a sense of failure, some would feel obliged to defend themselves and their son, and others would respond angrily to the perceived criticism.

Some parents avoid raising concerns with teachers in case the latter take this as a personal criticism. Parents may worry that their 'interference' could somehow rebound on their child.

While the teachers see a student's public image over a number of years, parents see the private side (which may be quite different) and have known their children intimately *throughout* their life. It is only when you put *both* views together that you get a complete picture.

The best possible thing for children is to feel that parents and teachers are working together, that there is no divide or tension between the two worlds they inhabit. This will not happen as a matter of course but requires work and commitment on both sides.

> *I listen very carefully to what parents say because they know their children better than anyone.*
> Sue Sanderson, Primary Headteacher

Parents can find it unhelpful to be given advice on what to do at home when this is based on lack of knowledge or understanding of their particular circumstances.

Examples

Teacher says: *He should read to you every day.*

Parent thinks: Great in theory! But by the time I've walked him home from school, collected his sister from the child minder, got tea, fed the family, bathed them and got them ready for bed, the evening's gone. If I keep him up any later he'll never get up in the morning.

Teacher says: *Can you make sure he does his homework?*

Parent thinks: I've been at work all day, I get home tired and just want to stop for a while. The last thing I feel like is another fight to go with 'do your chores', 'tidy your room', 'be in by 9 p.m.'. I want a relationship with my son, not to nag him all the time.

From a parent's point of view, communication with their child's teacher can be potentially fraught and laden with emotion. So what is the situation from a teacher's point of view?

Teachers' perceptions

Teachers are under a lot of pressure. Most work 'full-on' with around thirty pupils every day, and in secondary schools may teach two hundred different pupils over the week. Parents' meetings can be draining after a day's teaching, especially when scheduled after every school day throughout a week. To a tired teacher, a parent asking to meet outside of these times can sometimes seem:

— demanding
— interfering
— critical
— wanting exceptional treatment for their child

When there is criticism, teachers can take it personally and defend what has taken place. Their stance may be 'We are the professionals, we know best'.

Teachers can also find themselves in the difficult position of hearing one of their colleagues criticised. Understandably they may find it daunting to pass this feedback on. It may be easier to defend a colleague than listen to both sides of the story and help find a satisfactory way forward. A natural response to criticism is to grow defensive, but this will make it difficult to come up with solutions that satisfy both parties.

Time pressures

Both parents and teachers can be under a great deal of time pressure. As it becomes more common for both mothers and fathers to work, it is often difficult for parents with concerns to drop in during or at the end of a school day. Since teachers have to spend a large amount of time out of class on administration, preparation, marking and meetings, difficulties in catching parents to make arrangements to meet can make staying in contact seem like an extra burden.

The guidelines that follow will make your conversations with parents more productive, allowing you to address problems whilst they are relatively minor and reducing the emotion experienced on both sides.

How to get the best out of parents

- Recognise you are on the same side
- Listen to and acknowledge their concerns
- Use questions to find out more
- Describe their son's positive characteristics and achievements
- Be very specific about any problems, avoid generalisations and labels
- State what the student needs to do, rather than what he isn't doing
- Agree a plan of action and a time to review it

Recognise you are on the same side

Parents and teachers meet to discuss the progress of a pupil. Between them, they have a considerable effect on that child's life and how he performs at school. When parents and teachers discuss a boy's progress or behaviour, they generally both want the following things for that boy:

- his well-being and education
- his success
- good behaviour
- positive learning experiences

It is important that these common desires are recognised, and that everything you do gives the message 'we are here as equals to discuss the way forward for this student'. The message to the parent should be one of respect, and the following things can help establish this:

— be ready for a meeting with appropriate records and information
— be on time for a meeting
— have the room ready for a meeting with chairs and tables set out appropriately
— arrange for the parent to be greeted and taken to the meeting room
— if you have not met the parents before, introduce yourself by name and tell them your role
— thank them for having made time to come
— make them feel welcome, offer refreshments if the meeting is likely to be long
— tell them the purpose of the meeting
— avoid jargon and explain educational terms and procedures

Even if parents have come to a meeting because of their son's misdemeanour, remain friendly and positive. After all, it is the boy who has misbehaved, not the parents. They are simply there to help resolve the problem. It is unhelpful to pass (even unspoken) judgement on the parent, since this causes resentment, both in the short and long-term.

> **If you treat parents as though they are on the same side as you, they are likely to behave as though they are.**

CASE STUDY

The power of judgement
It was Christmas, and the time of the school performances. The mother took her five-year-old son back to school in the evening,

dropped him in his classroom to get ready and went to the hall to take a seat. The children came in, they did the performance, and she had a lump in her throat and watery eyes as she watched her first-born and his classmates on stage.

Performance over, the Headteacher thanked the children and their teachers and asked the parents to stay seated for the next performance. The boy's class filed out of the room. The next class started its performance. After a little while the mother began to wonder where her son was whilst this was going on. She supposed the teachers were looking after him. But the more she thought about it the more she realised that she didn't know. This was all new to her: supposing she should have picked him up after the performance, supposing all the other children had been picked up and he was the only one left. Each minute of the performance seemed endless and she finally crept out of the hall and headed to his classroom. To her huge relief, there was her son with a group of other children sitting on the carpet being read a story by a teacher she did not know.

'I've come for my son,' she said, 'Come on, sweetheart, we are going home now.' But he didn't want to go home yet, he wanted to hear the end of the story. No problem, she thought, I'm only here because I wanted to know he was safe, and he is.

'O.K.,' she said, 'I'll listen to the story with you,' and sat down, relieved that her panic was over. The teacher turned to the boy and said, 'You've got your mummy wrapped around your little finger, haven't you?' then continued to read the story. For the second time that evening the mother's emotions stopped her from listening to a word of what was going on. In the school hall the emotion had been panic, in her son's classroom it was humiliation.

If the mother arrived at school that evening without 'emotional baggage', she may have left with some. The teacher's comment, probably said with the intention of improving the boy, is likely to have affected the mother's relationship with the school over the next seven years.

Beware of passing judgement; you may only have part of the story.

When arranging a meeting with parents, consider whether it would be helpful for the boy to attend. Since his teacher and his parents are key adults in his life, he may find it overwhelming to have them both together. On the other hand it may be useful for you all to discuss his progress and to agree on the way forward. The best solution might be to have a frank conversation between adults first, where both sides have the opportunity to raise concerns that they may not want the boy to hear, then invite the boy to join you later. It may actually be very good for a child to see his parents and teachers talking reasonably together, especially where there have been any tensions between them in the past.

Sometimes meetings with parents get difficult and, when they do, parent-teacher communication can seem like a battle. Both parties want to stand their ground, not wanting to be seen to back down. It is essential to remember that, however it feels or looks, teachers and parents generally want the same thing: for the child to succeed. State at the outset of a conversation that you are on the same side, and restate it if the meeting gets a bit sticky.

Experts in negotiation point out the dangers of coming to a meeting with certain positions.[1] It is more effective, they say, to explore the interests of all parties.

Avoid positions, explore interests

At its simplest, the teacher's position may be 'Your son is wrong', and the parent's position may be 'You, the teacher, are wrong'. Positions such as these are likely to lead to defensiveness from both parties and are unlikely to encourage listening or a useful exchange of views. The exploration of interests, on the other hand, demonstrates a genuine desire to understand the other person's point of view and to explain your own.

Example

Instead of: Your son is not applying himself.

say: *I've been wondering how to get your son more interested in the subject. Do you have any ideas?*

Don't be surprised if parents defend their child – after all, if they don't, who will? It would be more surprising if they did not. Do not, however, fall into the trap of defending yourself. Defence often makes the other party want to attack further.

Don't defend, just explain

Example

Parent:	My son finds your subject boring.

Teacher:

Instead of:	He is the only one in the class who does.
say:	*That's a shame. I've taught this topic for three years and in the past it's gone down quite well.*

A good way to avoid being defensive is to put your attention on trying to understand fully the parents' point of view. In the example above the teacher might continue by saying: *What in particular does he find boring?*

Listen to and acknowledge parents' concerns

Few parents would make a special effort to speak to a teacher if they didn't have a concern (even if the concern is 'I don't know the person who is teaching my child'). Many parents lead busy lives, some feel uncomfortable in the school environment, and most are aware of the pressures on teachers and would not want to waste your time.

CASE STUDY

David was born in August. He was a cheerful and sociable child and got on well in Lower and Middle School. He was just 13 when he started Year 9 at the Upper School. By halfway through that year he found he was not able to keep up. He felt lost and started falling behind his classmates.

David developed eczema, was nervous and depressed at home and dreaded going to school. In the morning he often felt bad and would go in at lunchtime or take the day off. The doctor said it was a clear case of 'school-itis' and there was nothing he could do to help. David's mother explained the problem to his tutor and phoned him every time David was going to be late or off school. When David did go to school, however, he did not admit to having any difficulties and was quiet, smiling and good-natured.

Each term David's mother arranged to meet the tutor to discuss the problem. David attended these meetings but found it difficult to express how he felt. When his mother tried to explain on his behalf, she felt she was perceived as dominating her son. She suggested David dropped back a year to give himself a chance; he had plenty of friends in the year below so it would cause no social problems. The tutor did not see the need for such a drastic solution and recommended that David stayed with his current year. The mother, feeling that the tutor was a professional who probably knew best, agreed.

The problem continued throughout Year 10. The mother asked to see the Head of Year and suggested David should either drop back a year or do fewer GCSEs. The Head of Year saw no need for either course of action. The mother felt she was viewed as a neurotic single mother and started to wonder if she was.

In Year 11, David's GCSE year, his mother was so worried at the distress he displayed at home that she asked for an appointment with the Headteacher. Instead, an appointment was made for David and his mother to meet the tutor and the head of year. The teachers realised that the situation was now serious and came to the meeting with some options. Would David like to do fewer GCSEs, drop back a year, attend another school part time or change schools? David responded with non-committal grunts. His mother could see he was numb and that they had lost him. His tutor and the Head of Year left the mother and son to make a decision.

'I'm going home,' said David when they were alone, 'and I'm never coming back.' His mother arranged extended work experience for the rest of the year and David did not return to school or take any GCSEs.

In the case study above the parent did not feel heard or respected by the teachers with whom she dealt. One leads to the other, of course: if she had felt heard, she would also have felt respected. Many of the communication courses I run with businesses include a section on listening; and I have often asked to what degree individuals have felt listened to in life. Sadly, the majority of those I ask have felt disregard from others, and rarely thought they had been heard. Likely reactions to this are shown in the diagram below.

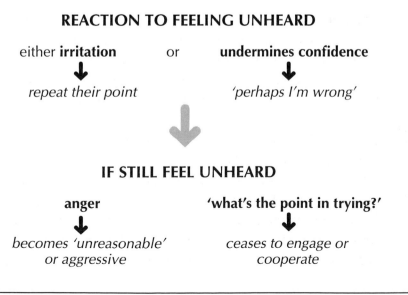

REACTION TO FEELING UNHEARD

either **irritation**　　　or　　　**undermines confidence**

⬇　　　　　　　　　　⬇

repeat their point　　　*'perhaps I'm wrong'*

⬇

IF STILL FEEL UNHEARD

anger　　　　　**'what's the point in trying?'**

⬇　　　　　　　　　　⬇

becomes 'unreasonable'　　　*ceases to engage or*
or aggressive　　　　　　　*cooperate*

Whether a parent's reaction to feeling unheard is irritation and anger or shutting down, the result is the same: a withdrawal of cooperation.

Because many people feel unheard, on the occasions they come across someone who *does* listen to and acknowledge the validity of their experience, they are often willing to trust and respect that listener. To create trust:

- **LISTEN** to their point of view
- **ACKNOWLEDGE** their point of view (remember, this does not imply agreement)
- **MAKE NOTES** of important points
- **SUMMARISE YOUR UNDERSTANDING** of their views

It is essential that parents' views be taken seriously.

Example

Parent:	My son has no time to play after school because he always has so much homework. He's a child, he needs time to play!
Teacher:	
Instead of:	Homework is very important, especially coming up to S.A.T.S.
say:	*So you are concerned he doesn't get enough time to play.*

When a person is feeling emotional, they are unable to think rationally, so it is unwise to try to 'reason' with upset parents, in fact it is likely to make things worse. Instead acknowledge how they might be feeling. Once the feelings are acknowledged the conversation will be able to move on.

Example

Parent:	My son missed the bus yesterday and when I phoned the school to find out what had happened I got an ansaphone. That's no way to run a school, it's disgraceful!
Teacher:	
Instead of:	The school secretary leaves at four o'clock and all the teachers were in a staff meeting.
say:	*It must have been worrying not to have had anyone available to speak to. The school secretary leaves at four o'clock and all the teachers were in a staff meeting.*

If a parent has worries or fears, you may be able to allay them, but only if the parent feels their concerns are being taken seriously. If they do not, any attempt to allay that fear will feel patronising.

Example

Parent:	David is getting very stressed about school. He can't keep up in most of the lessons and is falling behind. He doesn't want to come to school in the mornings and has developed eczema.
Teacher:	
Instead of:	There is nothing to worry about Mrs. Roberts, I have spoken to his subject teachers and they are satisfied with his work.
say:	*From what you are saying, Mrs. Roberts, it sounds as though David is not at all happy at the moment, we clearly need to rectify this. I've spoken to his subject teachers and they've each told me how he is doing and his predicted grades. Would it be useful if we looked at each subject, one by one?*

CASE STUDY

When they first started school the children attended for mornings only and after five weeks most would come for the full day. However any child who did not seem ready for full days could remain part-time for a bit longer. Three boys in the reception class did not seem ready for full-time schooling and their parents were asked to pick them up at lunchtime for a few more weeks. The father of one boy was incensed about this, feeling that his son was being disadvantaged right at the beginning of his school career.

When he complained to the teacher, she thought her professional judgement was being questioned and, knowing the child would be better off left free to run around in the afternoon, reiterated the recommendation. This angered the father further and he insisted on seeing the Headteacher. The teacher knew the Head agreed that the boy was not ready for full days and expected support for her recommendation.

To her surprise, the Head suggested to the father that the boy start full-time, with the option of going back part-time if it was clear to all that full-time was not right for him at this stage. Feeling somewhat undermined, the teacher queried the outcome: hadn't the Head submitted to the father's pressure, weren't they backing down?

'It may seem like that,' said the Head, 'but allowing him to go full-time does not mean your professional judgement was wrong, it simply demonstrates that we listened to his father's concerns and as a result were prepared to change our mind.'

Words like 'submit' and 'back down' reflect a 'them and us' mentality. It is more useful to think in terms of partnership, mutual benefit and exchange of views.

It is worth considering the parents' perception of the balance of power in the parent-teacher relationship. From a parent's point of view, it can seem that when things go wrong the odds are stacked heavily against them. This is why some parents feel they have to make a lot of noise in order to get what they perceive as justice. If parents thought that their concerns were being heard and acted upon, it is unlikely that they would feel the need to make a fuss.

Use questions to find out more

Meeting a parent provides an opportunity to find out more about a pupil – his interests, desires and concerns, what he is like at home and how he is responding to school. All this will give you a fuller picture. His parents have had to find strategies to motivate him since he was young, so it is a good idea to find out what works for them and ask them whether they think a similar approach might work at school.

If a parent has a criticism or complaint, ask questions to find out the exact nature of the problem. Not only does this give you more information, but parents will also feel that they are being taken seriously.

Example

'You say your son finds English boring and doesn't like the way it is taught. Do you know what in particular he doesn't like?'

Describe their son's positive characteristics and achievements

It is essential that parents hear about the positive aspects of their children. Not only is it encouraging for them as parents, but it also gives them something motivating to report back to their child. If you first tell them what their son does well, they will find it easier to accept any improvements you later suggest.

Example

'He produces excellent pieces of art that display a lot of imagination.' (Then, if necessary) *'I'd like to hear less chatting from him in class.'*

Remember to acknowledge small steps in the right direction:

Example

'Sam is learning to put his hand up rather than shouting out.'

Positive planning

Faber and Mazlish[2] tell of a teacher who contacts parents at the beginning of the school year when he knows students' behaviour will be at its best. He phones two parents a night to tell them something positive about their child. The time and money invested in establishing a good relationship is likely to pay off later in the year, since if he needs to contact a parent about a problem he knows the lines of communication are already open.

As a rule of thumb, let's say about 80% of students are performing satisfactorily about 80% of the time. If this is the case, it should not be difficult to find a lot of positive things to say about most of the students you teach. Even the 20% who fall below the 80%

satisfaction rate will, for a certain proportion of time, be attending lessons, conforming to school rules and producing work.

When reporting back to a parent it is important that they get the full story, what a student is doing right as well as what he is doing wrong.

Some parents who get negative reports from school punish their child. I heard of a fifteen-year-old boy who was on report for the last two weeks of term for being rude to teachers. His father was so angry when he was told this that he grounded his son for the whole of the Easter holidays. Whilst it is good to have parental support, a double punishment can be counterproductive.

Be specific about any problems, avoid generalisations and labels

When you give parents feedback about their child, it is important to be specific. Otherwise they are left with a general label for their child that they cannot do much with. The more detailed and specific the feedback you give them, the more able they will be to tackle problems with their child.

Examples

Instead of: He's disorganised.
say: *He often comes to lessons without everything he needs.*

Instead of: He's lazy.
say: *It takes a while before he settles and he seldom finishes a task in the time set.*

Instead of: He's disruptive.
say: *He often shouts out instead of putting his hand up.*

Instead of: He's violent.
say: *He hit a boy in the face at lunchtime, and this has happened on a few previous occasions when he gets upset. We need to help him find other ways of dealing with problems.*

When there are problems with a student, make sure the parent is kept informed and told about them before they become serious. Most problems develop gradually, so a parent should not expect to be faced with a surprise. Parents can be told about small problems in a note or a phone call.

Examples

A note:

> Dear Mr. and Mrs. Smith,
>
> I am concerned that John has not handed in any English homework for two weeks. Please could you make sure he does so in future. If there are any problems I would be happy to discuss them.
>
> Yours sincerely,
> Mrs. Jones, Class Teacher

A phone call:

'Hello, Mrs Smith? This is Mrs. Jones, John's class teacher. I'm a bit concerned because John has not handed in any English homework for two weeks. Were you aware of this?'

State what the student needs to do rather than what he isn't doing

It is more productive to point out a solution to a student than to dwell on the problem: the same applies to parents. Not only is this more encouraging for them, but it also gives them something with which to encourage their son.

Examples

- *'I'd like him to make sure he brings what he needs for each lesson.'*
- *'His work would improve significantly if he started each task immediately and worked steadily to finish it within the time set.'*

– *'He needs to put his hand up if he has a contribution and wait until he is chosen.'*

Agree a plan of action and a time to review it

Once you are confident that parents feel their point of view has been heard and any questions answered, you are in a position to explore options for a way forward. This should be a joint exercise, seeking a mutually satisfactory solution.

Explore options together, being as flexible and imaginative as you can. If you have a proposed course of action, set out the reasons and benefits clearly. The parent is more likely to understand and accept your suggestion if you first explain the reasons for it and afterwards describe the benefits of this course of action.

1. Explain the REASONS for your proposal.

2. Outline your PROPOSAL.

3. Point out the BENEFITS of this course of action.

Examples

Instead of: He will be given extra homework until he catches up.

say: *This is the only subject he is behind in, and with a little extra work he should be able to catch up. I'd like to set him some extra homework each week until he does. I think he will feel a lot better about himself, and the subject, once he's caught up with the rest of the class.*

Instead of: He will be suspended until half-term.

say: *He needs some time to cool off, and it is important that he and the other students understand that this sort of behaviour is unacceptable. I have suggested to the Head that he be suspended until half-term. We would provide work for him to do at home and he would probably find it easier to knuckle down without his friends to distract him.*

To get the parents on board, ask for their point of view and wherever possible offer them a choice.

Examples

- *'How you think he will respond to this?'*
- *'How do you feel about that?'*
- *'I'd appreciate your views on this.'*
- *'So he can either reduce the number of GCSEs he's taking or drop back a year: do you have a sense of what would work best for him?'*

Once a solution has been agreed upon, arrange a time to review it and make it a priority to implement everything you have agreed.

CASE STUDY

There were 44 children in Year 3, so it was decided to split the class into two groups of 22 in the mornings for academic work with a qualified teacher for each group, and combine them in the afternoons for practical subjects with a qualified teacher and a classroom assistant. Ostensibly the class was split by age, and the pupils referred to the two groups as 'the older children' and 'younger children'.

Daniel, whose birthday was in September was in the 'younger group'. He did not understand why he was not with his friends, and told his parents that he found school boring.

At Parents' Evening they asked how the class had been split. The teacher explained that it was to do with speed of delivery of the information being taught. Most of the children in the 'slower delivery' group were the younger ones, plus one or two, like Daniel, who they felt would cope better if the delivery were at the slower pace. She told them that in class he was quiet, day-dreamy and slow, and stumbled when reading aloud. This was a revelation, since at home he was loud, talkative, imaginative, constantly in motion and, although he resisted reading, reasonably fluent when pushed.

After the meeting his parents spoke to Daniel about what had been said and told him why he was with the younger children. He explained that he worked slowly because he was bored, that he had exciting adventures while day-dreaming and that he pretended not to read well because it was fun to trick the teacher. They pointed out that all these things made the teachers conclude that he should be in the slower group, which was why he was finding it so boring. They discussed what he would have to do to get into the faster group and set up another meeting with the teacher.

At the meeting they asked what Daniel would need to do to move into the other group. The teacher told them, and they set a target for Daniel to change groups in six weeks, agreeing to review progress in a month. At the review meeting the teacher reported encouraging improvements and Daniel joined the faster group on the target date.

Conclusion: a flexible solution

Flexibility on all sides will often lead to solutions that most help students. Sometimes to achieve this one may need to give up cherished ideas, but, if a student is happier as a result, the solution is likely to work out for the best. The following is one example of this.

CASE STUDY

Unbeknown to his parents and teachers, Jon had been bullied throughout secondary school, and by Year 10 was getting mixed up in drugs. One day he arrived home in a state of crisis. He refused to tell his parents what was going on, but was adamant that he would not go back to school. For the next three weeks he remained in this state.

Finally he asked if he could continue his studies at home. His parents were willing and able to tutor him, so they arranged a meeting with the Head to discuss it. They thought that they were going to the meeting to tell him they were withdrawing their son from school, and so were surprised at his response.

'Of course you can teach him at home,' he said, 'but I have a proposal to make. I would like you to leave him on the school roll, and then we will be able to provide you with all the support you need to get him through his GCSEs. To be frank, it helps us if you leave him on roll, he's worth about £2000 a year to us. But for that we would be able to provide him with books, mark his work and arrange all his exams for him. That would take a lot of the burden off you.'

At a later meeting the Head advised on what subjects Jon should take. It would be too much, he suggested, to continue with the eight GSCEs he had been studying, and far better to concentrate on five and get some good grades. The parents queried whether Jon shouldn't have a foreign language. In this case the Head felt not, it would put an unnecessary pressure on Jon, and five was the magic number should he ever want to go to university.

The parents took the Head's advice and, after being tutored at home for a year and a half, Jon emerged with five GCSEs – an 'A', two 'B's and two 'C's. He went out to work and at 19 saved up and travelled to South America.

Eighteen months later he returned fluent in Spanish and determined to go to university. His five GCSEs were sufficient to enrol him in an access course and a year later he had enrolled for a degree course in Spanish and European Studies. The Head was right, the mother thought, I didn't need to worry about Jon not having a foreign language.

Chapter summary

How to get the best out of parents

Recognise you are on the same side

- Demonstrate respect in all the messages you give
- Do not judge, you may not have the full story
- Explore interests rather than take a position
- Avoid defending, just explain

Listen to and acknowledge their concerns

- Listen to their point of view
- Acknowledge their point of view
- Instead of reasoning with upset parents, acknowledge their feelings
- Summarise your understanding of their views

Use questions to find out more

- Find out what the boy is like at home
- Ask how he is responding to school
- Seek to understand the exact nature of a problem

Describe their son's positive characteristics and achievements

- Start the conversation on a positive note
- State what the boy does well
- Acknowledge small steps in the right direction
- Contact parents with good news

Be very specific about any problems

♦ Clearly describe any problem areas
♦ Avoid generalisations and labels
♦ Do not wait for a problem to be serious before informing parents
♦ Focus on what the student needs to do, rather than what he isn't doing

Agree a plan of action and a time to review it

♦ Look for win-win solutions
♦ Outline reasons before suggesting a solution
♦ Get the parents to 'buy-in'
♦ Follow through on any actions you have agreed
♦ Meet again after a period to review the solution

Tomorrow's Men, Husbands and Fathers

If boys fail in school what effect will that have on their futures? Already young men have no guarantee of jobs and when they start a family they are not certain to be the breadwinners. On one hand crime and suicide are on the increase among young men and domestic violence is still common, on the other hand fathers are expected to spend more time with their children and play a larger part in child-rearing. If boys are disaffected at school, have poor qualifications and worse job prospects than women, then the future for them, their partners and their children is bleak.

When I was at school in the 1960s it was a radical idea that girls should achieve as much as boys, either at school or in the workplace. That vision, however, has become reality: the commitment of the teaching profession to equal opportunities over the last thirty years has allowed girls to shine at school and women to achieve as much as men in many areas.

Now the attention is on boys, and it requires the same degree of commitment from the teaching profession to enable this generation of boys to become the kind of men, partners, husbands and fathers that we would like to have in society. So what must we do for boys to enable them to thrive in the world in which they find themselves?

Firstly, we must value male attributes of energy, boldness, humour, competition, risk-taking and creativity.

Secondly, we must ensure that boys value themselves, knowing that they are able people, worthy of respect and admiration.

Thirdly, we must give them the skills to prepare them for adolescence and manhood. These include:

— *emotional literacy,* the ability to recognise their own feelings and those of others
— *communication,* the ability to express their ideas, thoughts and feelings constructively
— *self-discipline,* the ability to set their own boundaries and channel their own energy

If we succeed in these areas, then our boys will grow into men who feel valued by society and want to make their contribution to it, who show respect for other men and women, in particular their partners, who recognise and appreciate their own sons' energies and know how to bring the best out in them, and who are fathers that both their daughters and sons respect and admire.

A teacher can have an enormous effect on the way boys view themselves and, consequently, on how they behave. By valuing a boy and his qualities, they teach him to value himself; by respecting a boy, they teach him how to respect others; by channelling his energy, they teach him self-discipline; by teaching emotional literacy, they help boys express themselves fully, experience their emotions and develop emotional courage.

When teachers are able to bring the best out in the boys in their classrooms, they will have made an important contribution towards the creation of a stable, secure and loving society – now and in future generations.

If children live with criticism,
They learn to condemn.
If children live with hostility,
They learn to fight.
If children live with fear,
They learn to be apprehensive.
If children live with pity,
They learn to be sorry for themselves.
If children live with ridicule,
They learn to be shy.
If children live with jealousy
They learn what envy is.
If children live with shame,
They learn to feel guilty.

If children live with tolerance,
They learn to be patient.
If children live with encouragement
They learn to be confident.
If children live with praise,
They learn to appreciate.
If children live with approval,
They learn to like themselves.
If children live with acceptance,
They learn to find love in the world.
If children live with recognition,
They learn to have a goal.
If children live with sharing,
They learn to be generous.
If children live with honesty and fairness,
They learn what truth and justice are.
If children live with security,
They learn to have faith in themselves and in those around them.
If children live with friendliness
They learn that the world is a nice place in which to live.
If children live with serenity,
They learn to have peace of mind.

With what are your children living?

Dorothy L. Nolte[1]

Chapter Notes

Preface

1 Figures from Department for Education and Skills website: www.standards.dfee.gov.uk/genderandachievement
2 David Gillborn and Heidi Sfis Mirza (2000)
3 Tracey McVeigh: 'Boys lagging in class for years', *Guardian 23/9/01*

Chapter 1 Boys will be boys

1 S.Askew and C.Ross (1988); N. Browne and C. Ross (1991); S. Delamont (1990)
2 Unless stated otherwise information in this chapter referring to differences between boys' and girls' biology, behaviour or performance, and references to research, are drawn from Anne Moir & David Jessel: *BrainSex*.
3 Dan Kindlon and Michael Thompson (1999): *Raising Cain*
4 Scientists agree about where functions arc locatcd in the brain, but there is still some debate about how this affects behaviour and ability between the sexes. The following explanation is based on Moir and Jessel's summary of the working hypothesis that leading scientists now think most likely.

Whether people are good at something depends on the degree to which a particular part of the brain is devoted to that activity. The mechanics of language function is focused in only one part of the left hemisphere in girls but takes place in two parts of the left hemisphere in boys. This may explain why girls are likely to find grammar, spelling and punctuation easier than boys. The visio-spatial perception function takes place in the right hemisphere of the male brain and in both sides of the female brain. This may explain why boys are likely to be better at hand-eye coordination, map-reading, maths and construction than girls. There is also a hypothesis that the brain gets overloaded if asked to carry out too many functions at once. Hence the average male may find it easy to read a map and talk at the same time because these activities use different sides of the brain; the average female may prefer to do one of these activities at a time because each activity already uses both hemispheres, and doing both activities at the same time may create an overload.

5   Steve Biddulph (1998): *Raising Boys*

6   Steve Biddulph (1998): *Raising Boys*

7   Adrienne Katz, Ann Buchanan, Anne McCoy (1999): *Leading Lads*

8   Stephen Frosh, Ann Phoenix & Rob Pattman (2002): *Young Masculinities*

9   Don Foster: 'Mind the Gap' in *Education Journal,* May 1998

10 In the past parents knew they would have a place in their local school when their child reached five. Schools are now able to compete with one another for students, and parents must therefore try to get children into their preferred school. Living in the catchment area or a sibling attending a school no longer guarantees a child a place there, since infant schools are now restricted to no more than thirty pupils in a class, so those schools that have hit their quota are turning parents away.

11 Terry Goodkind (1995)

12 In *Adding value to boys' and girls' education* Madeleine Arnot and Jenifer Gubb looked at seven secondary schools where boys were making greater progress in value-added terms than girls, and at the strategies being used. They warn against becoming too structured and competitive which may put girls at a disadvantage.

Chapter 2 Valuing boys for who they are

1   Dan Kindlon and Michael Thompson: *Raising Cain*

2   Adele Faber and Elaine Mazlish (1995): *How To Talk So Kids Can Learn*

3   Adrienne Katz, Ann Buchanan and Anne McCoy: *Leading Lads*

Chapter 3 Allowing boys to be their best

1 Adrienne Katz, Ann Buchanan, Anne McCoy (1999): *Leading Lads*
2 In *Boys in Schools* (1995) by Rollo Browne and Richard Fletcher

Chapter 4 Giving boys an emotional vocabulary

1 Kevan Bleach: 'What difference does it make?' in *Raising Boys' Achievement in Schools*
2 In the *Making of Men* Mairtin Mac an Ghaill identifies a group of disaffected secondary school boys he calls the 'Macho Lads' who by Year 9 had rejected the official three Rs (reading, writing and arithmetic) and the unofficial three Rs (rules, routines and regulations) and opted for their own three Fs – fighting, fucking and football – as a way of surviving school authoritarianism and preparing themselves for the tough world outside. The boys reported arriving in the school believing in the three Rs and becoming disaffected during Years 7 and 8 by the need of the teachers to keep them down. Their disaffection might have been avoided had they experienced teachers using three Fs and one R: firmness, fairness, fun and respect.
3 Many schools use 'circle time' as a tool to raise children's self-esteem. See Resources page for details of how to introduce it.
4 Organised by Heartstone, a group promoting global citizenship. For details see Resources page.
5 For details of Life Education Centres see Resources page
6 See chapters 2 and 8 of Kevan Bleach (ed.): *Raising Boys' Achievement in Schools*

Review

1 This is based on a lesson a teacher asked me to give feedback on. Most of the things actually happened, some of the individual interventions were made by me rather than the teacher, some of the things are what I suggested the teacher could have said or done rather than what she did say or do.

Chapter 5 Channelling boys' energy

1   Kindlon and Thompson: *Raising Cain*

2   Kevan Bleach (1998) cites a study of 28 schools which concluded that boys are up to eight times more likely to be identified as having special needs as their female classmates.

3   Times Educational Supplement: 'Friday' Magazine, 30/3/01 review of Sue Cowley's *Getting the Buggers to Behave*

4   See Resources page

5   Gwenda Sanderson: 'Being Cool and a Reader' in Browne and Rollo (1995). Further suggestions of things boys like to read are given at the back of the book.

6   For more exercises see *Brain Gym, Teachers Edition* (1986) by P. and G. E. Dennison or Accelerated Learning in the Classroom by Alistair Smith

7   Article by Steve Biddulph: 'Do Boys Start School too Soon?' *The Melbourne Age*, 7/12/98

8   Steve Biddulph's *Raising Boys* explains how boys learn self-discipline through wrestling with adults, while Australian teachers and counsellors Maureen Moran and Annie McWilliam use wrestling as a way of getting physical with boys. (Maureen Moran 'Young and Powerful' in Browne and Rollo's *Boys in Schools*)

9   Geoff Hannan works with schools on classroom practices that allow both boys and girls to succeed. Contact details are in the Resources page.

10   Three of the chapters in *Raising Boys' Achievement in Schools,* ed. Kevan Bleach, explore this further.

11   Susan Siesage, 'Managing an improvement in boys' achievement at an inner city college', from a Dissertation for the MBA in Educational Management, University of Leicester, unpublished

12   From Jerome Burne: 'So you want better results? Try sitting boys next to girls.' *The Independent*, 5/4/01

13   www.schoolhouse.com has software to generate such worksheets.

Chapter 6 Boundaries and discipline

1   Susan Siesage, 'Managing an improvement in boys' achievement at an inner city college'

Chapter 7 Humour and playfulness

1   Times Educational Supplement: 'Friday' Magazine, 30/3/01
2   Faber and Mazlish: *How to Talk so Kids will Listen and Listen so Kids will Talk*

Chapter 9 Parents as allies

1   Roger Fisher and William Ury: *Getting to Yes*
2   Faber and Mazlish: *How to Talk so Kids will Learn*

Afterword: Tomorrow's men, husbands and fathers

1   In *Chicken Soup for the Soul, 101 Stories to Open the Heart and Rekindle the Spirit,* (1993) written and compiled by Jack Canfield and Mark Victor Hansen

Bibliography

Madeleine Arnot John Gray, Mary James, Jean Rudduck (1998): *Recent Research on Gender and Educational Performance* (OFSTED Reviews of Research), The Stationery Office, London

Madeleine Arnot and Jenifer Gubb (2001): *Adding Value to Boys' and Girls' Education, Gender and Achievement Project, West Sussex,* Cambridge University School of Education. The study is available from the INSET Office, West Sussex County Council, County Hall, Chichester PO19 1RF (01243 777100)

S. Askew and C. Ross (1988): *Why Boys Don't Cry − Boys and Sexism in Education,* Open University Press, Milton Keynes

Tom Baldwin, Pat Baldwin and Bernard Barker (1998): *Improving Boys' Performance,* Pearson Publishing

Steve Biddulph (1998): *Raising Boys,* Thorsons, London*

Steve Biddulph (1994): *Manhood,* Hawthorn Press, Stroud*

Kevan Bleach (ed.) (1998): *Raising Boys' Achievement in Schools,* Trentham Books, Stoke-on-Trent*

Kenneth Blanchard & Spencer Johnson (1982): *The One Minute Manager,* Fontana, Glasgow

R. Bray, P. Downes, C. Gardner, G. Hannan and N. Parsons (1997): *Can Boys do better?* Secondary Heads Association, Leicester

N. Browne and C. Ross (1991): 'Girls' Stuff, Boys' stuff: young children talking and playing' in N. Browne (ed.) *Science and Technology in the Early Years.* Open University Press, Milton Keynes

Rollo Browne and Richard Fletcher (1995): *Boys in Schools,* Finch Publishing, Sydney

Jack Canfield and Mark Victor Hansen (ed.) (1993): *Chicken Soup for the Soul,* 101 Stories to Open the Heart and Rekindle the Spirit, Health Communications, Deerfield Beach, Florida

Stephen Covey (1992): *Seven Habits of Highly Effective People,* Simon & Schuster, London

Sue Cowley (2001): *Getting the Buggers to Behave,* Continuum, London

Department of Education and Science (1989): *Discipline in Schools* (The Elton Report) HMSO, London

S. Delamont (1990): *Sex Roles and the School,* Methuen, London

P. and G. E. Dennison (1986): *Brain Gym, Teachers Edition.* Available from Body Balance Books, 12 Golders Rise, Hendon, London NW4 2HR. Tel: 020 8202 9547

Adele Faber and Elaine Mazlish (1995): *How to Talk so Kids can Learn,* Simon and Schuster*

Adele Faber and Elaine Mazlish (1980): *How to Talk so Kids will Listen,* Simon and Schuster

Anne Fines (1992): *Flour Babies,* Puffin, London*

Roger Fisher and William Ury (1981): *Getting to Yes,* Arrow Books, London

Stephen Frosh, Ann Phoenix & Rob Pattman (2002): *Young Masculinities,* Palgrave, Basingstoke

David Gillborn and Heidi Sfis Mirza (2000): *Educational Inequality: Mapping Race, Class and Gender – a synthesis of research evidence,* Ofsted, London

Daniel Golman (1996): *Emotional Intelligence,* Bloomsbury, London

Terry Goodkind (1995): *Wizard's First Rule,* Gollancz, London

John Gray (1992): *Men are from Mars and Women are from Venus,* Thorsons, London

Tim Kahn (1998): *Bringing up Boys,* Piccadilly Press, London

Adrienne Katz, Ann Buchanan and Anne McCoy (1999): *Leading Lads,* Young Voice, East Moseley

Dan Kindlon & Michael Thompson (1999): *Raising Cain,* Michael Joseph, London*

Mary Sheedy Kurcinka (1991): *Raising Your Spirited Child,* Harper Collins

Genie Z. Laborde (1983): *Influencing with Integrity,* Syntony Publishing, Palo Alto, California

Mairtin Mac an Ghaill (1994): *The Making of Men: masculinities, sexualities and schooling,* Open University Press, Buckingham

Dianne McGuinness (1985): *When Children Don't Learn,* Basic Books, New York

Anne Moir & David Jessel (1993): *BrainSex,* Mandarin, London

Lennard Nilson (1990): *A Child is Born,* Doubleday, London

Gwenda Sanderson (1995): 'Being Cool and a Reader' in Browne and Rollo in *Boys in Schools*

Susan Siesage (2001): 'Managing an Improvement in boys' Achievement at an inner city college', Extracts from a Dissertation for the MBA in Educational Management, University of Leicester, unpublished

Alistair Smith (1996): *Accelerated Learning in the Classroom,* Network Educational Press, Stafford

Dr. Gordon Thomas (1974): *Teacher Effectiveness Training,* Peter H. Lyden, New York

Mark Twain (1876): *The Adventures of Tom Sawyer,* Beehive Books, London

Marian Woodhall (1990): *How to Talk so Men will Listen,* Contemporary Books, Chicago

* recommended reading

Resources

Boys in schools

Neall Scott Partnership
Lucinda Neall and her colleagues provide 'Bringing out the Best in Boys' workshops, Inset days and classroom coaching for teachers.
4 Tornay Court, Church Road, Slapton, Leighton Buzzard,
Bedfordshire LU7 9BZ.
Tel: 01525 222600 E-mail: boys@neallscott.co.uk

Geoff Hannan Training
Programmes for teachers, young people and parents on Gender and Improving Teaching and Learning.
Book: *Improving Boys' Performance,* Reed International,
ISBN 0345 046268. Training Pack: ISBN 0435 016202
Interactive Video CD Rom: *Strategies for Improving Learning*
– available from TCI direct at Bank Cottage, Bourton Road, Much Wenlock, Shropshire TF13 6AJ. Tel: 01952 727332

Project JUDE
For details, contact Debra Myhill, Cathie Holden or Liz Wood at Exeter University, School of Education and Lifelong Learning, Heavitree Road, Exeter, EX1 2LU. E-mail: d.a.myhill@ex.ac.uk

Self-esteem & Emotional Literacy

Circle Time
Jenny Mosley Consultancies, 8 Westbourne Road, Trowbridge, Somerset BA14 04J. Tel: 01225 767157

Life Education Centres – helping children make healthy choices
1st Floor, 53-56 Great Sutton Street, London EC1V 0DG
Tel. 0207 490 3210 Website: www.lifeeducation.org.uk

Catherine Corrie runs workshops on how to create a supportive and exciting learning environment, focussing on the effect the inner state has on motivation, behaviour and success. Her book *Becoming Emotionally Intelligent* published by Network Educational Press will be available in Autumn 2002.
Tel: 0208 575 1505 E-mail: cath@wisechild.co.uk

Heartskills
35 Murray Road, Northwood, Middlesex HA6 2YP
Tel: 01923 820 900 E-mail: info@heartskills.com
Website: www.heartskills.com

Accelerated Learning

Alistair Smith
Alite, 45 Wycombe End, Beaconsfield HP9 1LZ
Tel: 01494 671444
E-mail: office@alite.co.uk Website: www.alite.co.uk

Brain Gym
Educational Kinaesiology Foundation, 12 Golders Rise, Hendon, London NW4 2HR. Tel: 020 8202 3141

Dr Eva Hoffman
Learn to Learn, PO Box 29, Middlewich, Cheshire CW10 9FN
Tel: 01606 832895 E-mail: learntolearn@connectfree.co.uk
Website: www.learntolearn.org.uk

Mind Motivation Ltd.
1st Floor, Tring House, 77 High Street, Tring, Hertfordshire
HP23 4AB. Tel: 01442 826748 E-mail: info@mindmotivation.com
Website: www.mindmotivation.com

Literacy

Alan Gibbon, author, offers author talks and workshops for
Years 3 – 8 and in-service training entitled: 'Boys – can't read,
won't read?' The Writing Classroom, c/o Prescot County Primary,
Maryville Road, Prescot, Merseyside L34 2TA
Tel: 0151 426 4842 E-mail: aagibbins@blueyonder.co.uk

Gavin Stewart, poet, runs in-service training on poetry and creative
writing,as well as a range of workshops and activities for primary
and secondary pupils.
53 Rowley Furrows, Linslade, Leighton Buzzard, Bedfordshire
Tel: 01525 376899 E-mail: stewartga@waitrose.com
Website: www.users.waitrose.com/~stewartga

Paula Taylorson runs poetry and creative writing workshops for
primary and secondary students and is working on a book of
poems for teenage boys for publication in 2003.
Tel: 01582 654806 E-mail: r.taylorson@ntlworld.com

Society of Storytellers
PO Box 2344, Reading RG6 7FG Tel: 0118 935 1381

Citizenship

Heartstone
Tel: 01349 865400 E-mail: info@heartstone.co.uk

Worksheets

Website: www.schoolhouse.com

Recommended Reading for Boys

We asked boys what kinds of things they like to read. This is what they said:

Magical Books   *Adventure Books*   *Animal Books*
Mystery Books   *Funny Books*   *Horror*
Fantasy   *Information books*   *Atlases*
Mythical Legends

These are the books they recommended, with those most suitable for younger readers higher up the list:

Non Fiction

'How' Books, Usborne
I Wonder Why Series, Kingfisher
'Eyewitness' Series, Dorling Kindersley
Joke Books
Observer Series, Penguin
History Detective Series by Philip Ardagh, Macmillan Children's Books
Horrible Histories Series by Terry Deary, Scholastic Hippo
Adventures from History Series Ladybird Books, Wills & Hepworth
Horrible Science by Nick Arnold, Scholastic Books
Just Stupid by Andy Griffiths, McMillan Children's Book
Guinness Book of Records, Gullane Publishing
Coping with School by Peter Corey, Scholastic
Boys Behaving Badly by Jeremy Daldry, Piccadilly Press
Comics, Newspapers and Magazines

Fiction

I Don't Want To by Bel Mooney, Mammouth

Elephants Don't Sit on Cars by David Henry Wilson, Macmillan Children's Books

Bad Boys by David Ross & Bob Cattle, Andre Deutsch

Horrible Henry by Francesca Simon, Dolphin

Greek Myths retold by Heather Amery, Usborne Publishing

I wish, I wish by Paul Shipton, Oxford Reading Tree

Mr Majeika by Humphrey Carpenter, Puffin

Stan's Dragon by Maggie Pearson, Hodder & Stoughton

The Twits by Roald Dahl, Puffin Books

Viking at School by Jeremy Strong, Puffin Books

Goosebumps Series by R.L. Stine, Scholastic Children's Books

Football Crazy by Patricia Borlenghi, Bloomsbury

The Bugalugs Bum Thief by Tim Winton, Puffin

Top Ten Greek Legends by Terry Deary, Scholastic

The Adventures of Junior James Bond by R D Mascott, Jonathan Cape Children's Books

The Odyssey retold by Barbara Leonie-Pickard, Oxford University Press

Captain Underpants by Dav Pilkey, Scholastic Books

King Arthur retold by James Riordan, Oxford University Press

Harry Potter by J K Rowling, Bloomsbury Children's Books

Mrs Frisby and the Rats from NIMH by Robert C O'Brien, Puffin Books

Scary Stories to Tell in the Dark by Alvin Schwartz, Lippincott, Williams & Wilkins

Ghost Dog by Elaneor Allen, Little Apple Books

Narnia Collection by C.S. Lewis, Puffin

Hardy Boys Mystery Stories by Franklin W. Dixon, Simon & Schuster Children's Books

I Was a Rat by Philip Pullman, Corgi Yearling

Scribbleboy by Philip Ridley, Puffin

Grandma Baa by Roger Hargreaves, Macmillan Children's Books

The Wind Singer by William Nicholson, Egmont Books

Gift of the Gab by Maurice Gleitzman, Puffin

The Saga of Darren Shan, Collins

Feather Boy by Nicky Singer, Collins

The Kite Rider by Geraldine McCaughrean, Oxford University Press

Hydra by Robert Swindells, Yearling

Kensuke's Kingdom by Michael Morpurgo, Mammoth

Cliffhanger by Jacqueline Wilson, Yearling Books

A Series of Unfortunate Adventures by Lemony Snicket, Egmont

Swallows and Amazons by Arthur Ransome, Random House Red Fox

The Number Devil by Hans Magnus Enzensberger, Granton Books

Point Blanc by Anthony Horowitz, Walkers Books

Wrecked by Robert Swindells, Puffin Books

Holes by Louis Sachar, Bloomsbury Children's Books

Face by Benjamin Zephaniah, Bloomsbury Children's Books

Unbelievable by Paul Jennings, Puffin

The Phantom Tollbooth by Norton Juster, Collins

Horowitz Horror by Anthony Horowitz, Orchard Books

Street Child by Berlie Doherty, Collins

Scupper Hargreaves, Football Genius by Chris d'Lacey, Corgi Yearling

The Shadow of the Minotaur Trilogy by Alan Gibbons, Orion Children's Books

War Boy by Michael Foreman, Puffin

Tales of Redwall by Brian Jaques, Red Fox

Worlds of Chrestimanci by Diana Wynne Jones, Collins

Flour Babies by Anne Fine, Puffin

The Silver Sword by Ian Serraillier, Puffin

Julie and Me...and Michael Owen Makes Three by Alan Gibbons, Orion Children's Books

The Dadhunters by Josephine Feeney, Collins

Artemis Fowl by Eoin Colfer, Penguin
Buffy the Vampire Slayer by Nancy Holder & Christopher Golden, Pocket Books
His Dark Materials Trilogy by Philip Pullman, Scholastic Children's Books
Lord of the Rings by J R R Tolkien, Harper Collins

Poetry
Silly Verse for Kids by Spike Milligan, Puffin Books
Please Mrs Butler by Allan Ahlberg, Puffin Books
Revolting Rhymes by Roald Dahl, Puffin Books
Beowulf translated by Seamus Heaney, Penguin
The Iron Wolf by Ted Hughes, Faber & Faber
Shortcuts and Teenage Ramblings by Patrick & Tim Chasslis, Balanced Books
Studying Poetry by Stephen Matterson & Darren Jones, Arnold Books

Reading Resources
www.guysread.com
www.ukchildrensbooks.co.uk
www.worldofdiscovery.com
www.lemonysnicket.com
www.darrenshan.com
www.poetryclass.net
www.poetrysociety.org.uk/education
www.amazon.co.uk

Statistics

Gender and Attainment

- Boys' performance is lower than girls' in all literacy-related tasks and tests in England. Girls outperform boys in reading throughout the western world at age 9.
- Girls were doing better than boys in the 11-plus exam four decades ago. A lower cut-off point was required for boys to ensure equal numbers of each gender went to grammar school.
- In 1999, at the end of Key Stage 3 (14 year olds), the significant gender difference in performance remained with 55% of boys in England achieving level 5 or above in comparison to 72% of girls.
- In 2001, 55.2% of 16 year-old girls in England passed 5 or more GCSEs at grade C or above compared to 44.6% of boys.
- Subject differences, 1999/2000: modern languages, 48% girls aged 15 achieved GCSE grade A*-C compared with 32% boys, and for English, this was 62% compared with 46%. Higher proportion of boys achieved GCSE grades A*-C in physics, chemistry, biology, IT and PE.
- Results for boys and girls differ considerably with school type. For 1998/99: **Comprehensive schools:** 39.7% of 15 year-old boys achieved 5+ A*-C GCSE grades, compared to 50.5% of girls. **Selective schools:** 95.5% boys achieved 5+ A*-C grades, girls 97.2%. **Modern schools:** boys 26.8%, girls 38.8%. **All maintained schools:** boys 39.9%, girls 51.0%. **Independent schools:** boys 77.7%, girls 84.5%.

(See Statistical Bulletin No. 04/2000 'GCSE/GNVQ and GCE A/AS Level and Advanced GNVQ Examination Results 1998/99 – England', DfEE May 2000)

- Of the 50,000 pupils leaving school in 1998 without any qualifications, 57% (28,500) were boys.
- In September 2000, 66% of boys compared with 73% of girls stayed on in full-time education beyond the statutory leaving age.
- In 2000, girls achieved more grade A passes than boys in A Levels, having trailed behind since these began in 1951.

(From DfEE and National Literacy Trust)

'We face a genuine problem of underachievement among boys, particularly those from working-class families. This underachievement is linked to a laddish culture which, in many areas, has grown out of deprivation and a lack of both self-confidence and opportunity.'
David Blunkett, then Education Secretary (in Rosemary Bennett, 'Mixed schools many go for single-sex classes', *Financial Times,* 21 August 2000)

2001 A-levels: girls achieved 0.8% more A grades (19% compared to 18.2%) and 1.9% more A-E grades (90% compared to 88.8%). **AS-Levels:** girls did 3,2% better at grade A (18.5% compared to 15.4 %) and 4.2% better at A-E (88.5% to 84.3%). (From DfEE)

Research at the University of Edinburgh:
'gender gap has existed for more than a quarter of a century but social class is the source of far more underachievement and inequality in schools than gender.'

'Historical trends in what children are achieving by the age of 16 show that levels of attainment of both girls and boys have risen substantially since 1965, but that the rise was greater for females. But within ten years there was lower average attainment by boys compared with girls.'
Tracy McVeigh, 'Boys lagging in class for years', *Guardian* 23 September 2001

Prof. Alan Smithers, Liverpool University: 'The crucial thing is that they are both improving but the girls are improving more.'
Will Woodward, 'Girls lead AS exam results', *Guardian* 16 August 2001

Exclusion

- Between 1995 and 1999, around 83% of all permanent exclusions were of boys.
- 1995/96 to 1997/98, about 27 in every 10,000 boys were excluded, dropping to 22 in every 10,000 in 1998/9. (rates for girls: 6 per 10,000 in 1995/96, 1996/97, and 5 per 10,000 in 1997/98 and 1998/99.)
- Most common age for exclusion is 14, and altogether nearly 8 out of 10 exclusions are of pupils aged 12-15.
- Far higher proportion of Black Caribbean, Black African and Black Other groups were excluded than of other ethnic groups. In 1997/98 the rate for Black Caribbean pupils was 4.5 times that for white pupils. (Lower proportions of Indian, Bangladeshi and Chinese ethnic groups were excluded than for other minorities.)
- 'Pupils with statements of SEN (special educational need) much more likely to be excluded from school than those who do not have statements. ....in 1996/97 1.11% of all pupils with statements of SEN were excluded from school compared to only 0.14% of rest of school population – the former rate being 8 times the latter. (Decrease in 1998/99 – 0.91% pupils with SEN compared 0.11% ie just over 7 times).

(From DFEE National Statistics Bulletin Issue No. 10/00 November 2000 'Statistics of Education: Permanent Exclusions from Maintained Schools in England'.)

Suicide

- 2 suicides every day by young people in UK and Ireland
- 80% of suicides are by young men

Rate of suicide amongst young men (15-24 years) in the UK has increased since the 1970s — statistics showed a downturn from 1993, but the rate rose once again in 1997 to 17 per 100,000, compared with a national suicide rate of 13 per 100,000 ...the rate in Scotland for young men continued to rise and is now 33 per 100,000.
(The Samaritans 'Young people and suicide' from
http://www.samaritans.org.uk/know/young_people.html)

'Although three times as many girls actually attempt suicide, boys are four times more likely to succeed'
Claire Wallerstein, 'You spend your whole time trying to understand why he chose death instead of life', *Guardian* 21 February 2002

'Unlike suicide deaths, which occur most frequently in men aged 25-34 and over 75, deliberate self-harm is most common among young women aged 15-19. Recently, however, researchers reported a large, sudden increase in suicide attempts by younger men and boys aged 15-24, whose rate nearly tripled between 1985 and 1995. The recent trend for females is also increasing...'.
(The Samaritans 'Attempted suicide' on
http://www.samaritans.org/know/attempted.html)

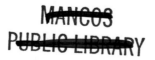

Other books from Hawthorn Press

Manhood
An action plan for changing men's lives

STEVE BIDDULPH

Steve Biddulph, author of *Raising Boys* and the million-seller *The Secret of Happy Children,* writes about the turning point that men have reached.

'Steve Biddulph should be in the UK what he is in Australia, the household name in the business of raising boys and being a man.' Dorothy Rowe, psychologist and writer

272pp; 216 x 138mm; 1 869 890 99 X; pb

Being a Parent
PARENT NETWORK

Being a parent is one of the most important jobs in the world, because parents hold the future in their hands. Parents need all the help they can get. Yet many battle on without any support or guidance. *Being a Parent* helps you think about what support you and your children need. It gives ideas on how to make family life a little easier.

'I consider this book and other Parent Network courses to have great value, because I believe that parents deserve all the help they can get...'
Alan Titchmarsh,TV and Radio Broadcaster, Author and Gardener

96pp; 297 x 210mm; 1 869 890 81 7; pb

Parenting Matters
Ways to bring up your children using heart and head

PARENT NETWORK

Parenting Matters helps you bring up loving and happy children. Here is the heart to becoming the more confident, sensitive relaxed, firm and caring parent that you truly are – enjoying your children and family.

'Parent Network courses have brought smiles to the faces, and deep sighs of relief to thousands of parents all over the UK. A chance to sort out your thinking and raise your kids in the way you really want to, instead of in a series of knee-jerk reactions.'
Steve Biddulph, family therapist and parenting author

228pp; 297 x 210mm; 1 869 890 16 7; pb

Ready to Learn
From Birth to School Readiness
MARTYN RAWSON AND MICHAEL ROSE

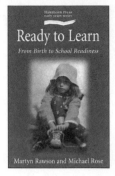

Ready to Learn will help you to decide when your child is ready to take the step from kindergarten to school proper. The key is an imaginative grasp of how children aged 0-6 years learn to play, speak, think and relate between birth and six years of age.

192pp; 216 x 138mm; 1 903458 15 3; pb

Getting in touch with Hawthorn Press

We would be delighted to hear your feedback on our Education books, how they can be improved, and what your needs are. Visit our website for details of the Education Series and forthcoming books and events: **www.hawthornpress.com**

Ordering books
If you have difficulties ordering Hawthorn Press books from a bookshop, you can order direct from:

United Kingdom
> Booksource Distribution
> 32 Finlas Street, Glasgow, G22 5DU
> Tel: 0141 558 1366 Fax: 0141 557 0189
> E-mail: orders@booksource.net
> Website: www.booksource.net

North America
> Anthroposophic Press c/o Books International
> PO Box 960, Herndon, VA 201 72-0960.
> Toll free order line: 800-856-8664
> Toll free fax line: 800-277-9747